Basic Computation Series

Applying Computational Skills

Loretta M. Taylor, Ed. D.

Harold D. Taylor, Ed. D.

Dale Seymour Publications®
Parsippany, New Jersey

Editorial Manager: Carolyn Coyle

Development Editor: Deborah J. Slade

Production/Manufacturing Director: Janet Yearian

Sr. Production/Manufacturing Coordinator: Roxanne Knoll

Design Director: Jim O'Shea

Design Manager: Jeff Kelly

Cover Designer: Monika Popowitz

Interior Designer: Christy Butterfield

This book is published by Dale Seymour Publications®, an imprint of Pearson Learning.

Dale Seymour Publications
299 Jefferson Road
Parsippany, NJ 07054-0480
Customer Service: 800-872-1100

ISBN 0-7690-0122-X
Order Number DS21924

1 2 3 4 5 6 7 8 9 10–ML–04 03 02 01 00

This Book Is Printed
On Recycled Paper

Authors of the Basic Computation Series 2000

Loretta M. Taylor is a retired high school mathematics teacher. During her teaching career, she taught at Hillsdale High School in San Mateo, California; Crestmoor High School in San Bruno, California; Patterson High School in Patterson, California; Round Valley Union High School in Covelo, California; and Farmington High School in Farmington, New Mexico. Dr. Taylor obtained a B.S. in mathematics from Southeastern Oklahoma State University, and both an M.A. in mathematics and an Ed.D. in mathematics education from the University of Northern Colorado. She has been active in professional organizations at the local, state, and national levels, including the National Council of Teachers of Mathematics, the California Mathematics Council, the National Education Association, and the California Teachers Association. She has given a variety of talks and workshops at numerous conferences, schools, and universities. Dr. Taylor is a member of Lambda Sigma Tau, a national honorary science fraternity, and is coauthor of *Paper and Scissors Polygons and More, Algebra Book 1, Algebra Book 2,* and *Developing Skills in Algebra 1.* In retirement, she continues to be an active mathematics author and is involved with community organizations.

Harold D. Taylor is a retired high school mathematics teacher, having taught at Aragon High School in San Mateo, California; as well as at Patterson High School in Patterson, California; Round Valley Union High School in Covelo, California; and Farmington High School in Farmington, New Mexico. He has served in high schools not only as a mathematics teacher, but also as a mathematics department head and as an assistant principal. He received a B.S. in mathematics from Southeastern Oklahoma State University, and both an M.A. in mathematics and an Ed.D. in mathematics education from the University of Northern Colorado. Dr. Taylor has been very active in a number of professional organizations, having worked in a variety of significant capacities for the National Council of Teachers of Mathematics and the California Mathematics Council. He was chairman of the Publicity and Information Committee and the Local Organizing Committee for the Fourth International Congress on Mathematics Education at Berkeley, California, was on the writing team of the California Assessment Test, and was a member of the California State Mathematics Framework and Criteria Committee, chairing the California State Mathematics Framework Addendum Committee. Since 1966, he has spoken at more than one hundred local, state, and national meetings on mathematics and mathematics education. Dr. Taylor is author of *Ten Mathematics Projects and Career Education Infusion,* and coauthor of *Algebra Book 1, Algebra Book 2,* and *Developing Skills in Algebra 1.* In 1989 he was the California recipient of the Presidential Award for Excellence in Teaching Secondary Mathematics. In retirement, Dr. Taylor is continuing to produce mathematics materials for the classroom, and also serves his community as County Judge in Custer County, Colorado, having been appointed to this position by Governor Roy Romer.

Table of Contents

A Note of Introduction

To the Teacher

Some students are familiar with computational work but have never really mastered it. Perhaps this is a result of a lack of practice. With the *Basic Computation Series 2000,* you can provide students with as much practice as they need. You can teach, check up, reteach, and reinforce. You can give class work and homework. If you wish, you can create a full year's course in basic computation, or you can provide skills maintenance when it's needed. All the work is here. Select the pages you want to use for the students who need them.

To the Student

You can't play a guitar before you learn the chords. You can't shoot a hook shot before you learn the lay-up. You can't pass a mathematics exam before you learn to compute, and you can't master computational skills until you learn the mathematical facts and procedures. Learning takes practice; there are no shortcuts. The pages in this book are for practice. Do your math every day and think about what you're doing. If you don't understand something, ask questions. Don't do too much work in your head; it's worth an extra sheet of paper to write down your steps. Also, be patient with yourself. Learning takes time.

Although calculators and other computational devices are readily available to most everyone, you will be forever handicapped if you are not able to perform basic mathematical computations without the aid of a mechanical or electronic computational device. Learn and master the procedures so that you can rely on your own abilities.

To the Parent

The importance of the development of mathematical skills cannot be emphasized enough. Mathematics is needed to estimate materials for a construction job or to price a car. It's needed to predict earthquakes and to prescribe medicine. It helps you determine how to stretch your dollars and pay your bills. This program provides the practice students need to develop the essential computational skills. Conventional algorithms are utilized throughout the *Basic Computation Series 2000.* You can help your children learn these skills. Give them your support and encouragement. Urge them to do their homework. Be there to answer their questions. Give them a quiet place to work. Make them feel good about trying. Your help can make the difference.

About the Program

What is the Basic Computation Series 2000?

The books in the *Basic Computation Series 2000* provide comprehensive practice on all the essential computational skills. There are nine practice books and a test book. The practice books consist of carefully sequenced drill worksheets organized in groups of five. The test book contains daily quizzes (160 quizzes in all), semester tests, and year-end tests written in standardized-test format.

Book 1	Working with Whole Numbers
Book 2	Understanding Fractions
Book 3	Working with Fractions
Book 4	Working with Decimals
Book 5	Working with Percents
Book 6	Understanding Measurement
Book 7	Working with Perimeter and Area
Book 8	Working with Surface Area and Volume
Book 9	Applying Computational Skills
Test Book 10	Basic Computation Quizzes and Tests

Who can use the Basic Computation Series 2000?

The *Basic Computation Series 2000* is appropriate for use by any person, young or old, who has not achieved computational proficiency. It may be used with any program calling for carefully sequenced computational practice. The material is especially suitable for use with students in fifth grade, middle school, junior high school, special education classes, and high school. It may be used by classroom teachers, substitute teachers, tutors, and parents. It is also useful for those in adult education, for those preparing for the General Education Development Test (GED), and for others wishing to study on their own.

What is in this book?

This book is a practice book. In addition to explanation and examples for the student, parent, and teacher, it contains student worksheets, answers, and a record sheet.

Worksheets

The worksheets are designed to give even the slowest student a chance to master the essential computational skills. Most worksheets come in five equivalent forms allowing for pretesting, practice, and post-testing on any particular skill. Each set of worksheets provides practice on only one or two specific skills, and the work progresses in very small steps from one set to the next. Instructions are clear and simple. Ample practice is provided on each page, giving students the opportunity to strengthen their skills. Answers to each problem are included in the back of the book.

Explanatory Material

The beginning of each section includes explanatory material designed to help students, parents, and teachers understand the material in the section and its purpose. Fully-worked examples show how to work each type of exercise. The example solutions are written in a straightforward manner so as to be easily understood.

Student Record Sheet

A record sheet is provided to help in recording progress and assessing instructional needs.

Answers

Answers to all problems are included in the back of the book.

How can the Basic Computation Series 2000 be used?

The materials in the *Basic Computation Series 2000* can serve as the major skeleton of a skills program or as supplements to any other computational skills program. The large number of worksheets provides a wide variety from which to choose and allows flexibility in structuring a program to meet individual needs. The following suggestions are offered to show how the *Basic Computation Series 2000* may be adapted to a particular situation.

Minimal Competency Practice

In various fields and schools, standardized tests are used for entrance, passage from one level to another, and certification of competency or proficiency prior to graduation. The materials in the *Basic Computation Series 2000* are particularly well-suited to preparing for any of the various mathematics competency tests, including the mathematics portion of the General Education Development Test (GED) used to certify high school equivalency.

Together, the books in the *Basic Computation Series 2000* provide practice on all the essential computational skills measured on competency tests. The semester tests and year-end tests from the test book are written in standardized-test format. These tests can be used as sample minimal competency tests. The worksheets can be used to brush up on skills measured by the competency tests.

Skills Maintenance

Since most worksheets come in five equivalent forms, the work can be organized into weekly units as suggested by the following schedule: A five-day schedule can begin on any day of the week. The authors' ideal schedule begins on Thursday, with pretesting and introduction of a skill, and follows with reteaching on Friday. Monday and Tuesday are for practice, touch-up teaching, reinforcing, and individualized instruction. Wednesday is test day. Daily quizzes from the *Basic Computation Series 2000 Quizzes And Tests Book* can be used on the drill-and-practice days for maintenance of previously-learned skills or diagnosis of skill deficiencies. Ideally, except for test days, a quiz may be given during the first fifteen minutes of a class period with the remainder of the period used for instruction and practice with other materials.

Authors' Suggested Teaching Schedule

	Day 1	Day 2	Day 3	Day 4	Day 5
Week 1	Pages 4 and 5 Pages 14 and 15	Pages 6 and 7 Pages 16 and 17	Pages 8 and 9 Pages 18 and 19	Pages 10 and 11 Pages 20 and 21	Pages 12 and 13 Pages 22 and 23
Week 2	Pages 29 and 30 Pages 39 and 40	Pages 31 and 32 Pages 41 and 42	Pages 33 and 34 Pages 43 and 44	Pages 35 and 36 Pages 45 and 46	Pages 37 and 38 Pages 47 and 48
Week 3	Pages 49 and 50 Pages 59 and 60	Pages 51 and 52 Pages 61 and 62	Pages 53 and 54 Pages 63 and 64	Pages 55 and 56 Pages 65 and 66	Pages 57 and 58 Pages 67 and 68
Week 4	Pages 71 and 72 Pages 81 and 82	Pages 73 and 74 Pages 83 and 84	Pages 75 and 76 Pages 85 and 86	Pages 77 and 78 Pages 87 and 88	Pages 79 and 80 Pages 89 and 90
Week 5	Pages 93 and 94 Pages 103 and 104	Pages 95 and 96 Pages 105 and 106	Pages 97 and 98 Pages 107 and 108	Pages 99 and 100 Pages 109 and 110	Pages 101 and 102 Pages 111 and 112

Supplementary Drill

There are more than 18,000 problems in the *Basic Computation Series 2000*. When students need more practice with a given skill, use the appropriate worksheets from the series. They are suitable for classwork or homework practice following the teaching of a specific skill. With five equivalent pages for most worksheets, adequate practice is provided for each essential skill.

How are the materials prepared?

The books are designed with pages that can be easily reproduced. Permanent transparencies can be produced using a copy machine and special transparencies designed for this purpose. The program will run more smoothly if the student's work is stored in folders. Record sheets can be attached to the folders so that students, teachers, or parents can keep records of an individual's progress. Materials stored in this way are readily available for conferences with the student or parent.

Student Record Sheet

Worksheets Completed

Page Number

4	6	8	10		12
5	7	9	11		13
14	16	18	20		22
15	17	19	21		23
29	31	33	35		37
30	32	34	36		38
39	41	43	45		47
40	42	44	46		48
49	51	53	55		57
50	52	54	56		58
59	61	63	65		67
60	62	64	66		68
71	73	75	77		79
72	74	76	78		80
81	83	85	87		89
82	84	86	88		90
93	95	97	99		101
94	96	98	100		102
103	105	107	109		111
104	106	108	110		112

Quiz Grades

No.	Score

Checklist

Skill Mastered	Date
❑ sequences	_____
❑ averages	_____
❑ income tax and sales tax	_____
❑ squares and square roots	_____
❑ reading bar graphs	_____
❑ reading line graphs	_____
❑ constructing bar graphs	_____
❑ constructing line graphs	_____
❑ reading circle graphs	_____
❑ constructing circle graphs	_____
❑ reading maps	_____
❑ making change	_____
❑ comparing unit prices	_____
❑ word problems	_____
❑ evaluating information	_____
❑ estimation	_____

Notes _____

_____

_____

_____

_____

Sequences, Averages, and Tables

A *sequence* is a set of numbers in a specific order that forms a pattern. Sometimes the pattern is easy to determine, in other cases, it is not. To determine the pattern, the given numbers should be studied for clues as to their relationship to each other. Finding the pattern for a sequence often requires trial and error.

Example 1: Fill in the blanks by following the pattern.

9, 18, 27, 36, ___, ___, ___, ___, ___, ___, ___, ___, ___, ___, ___, ___

Solution: Since 9, 18, 27, and 36 are consecutive multiples of 9, the numbers that complete the sequence are 45, 54, 63, 72, 81, 90, 99, 108, 117, 126, 135, and 144.

Example 2: Fill in the blanks by following the pattern.

6, 11, 16, 21, ___, ___, ___, ___, ___, ___, ___, ___, ___, ___, ___, ___

Solution: The given numbers are not multiples of any particular whole number, but a clue to the pattern is that the numbers are 5 apart. This suggests that the numbers in the sequence are related to multiples of 5. In fact, each number is one more than a multiple of 5. Thus, the numbers that complete the sequence are 26, 31, 36, 41, 46, 51, 56, 61, 66, 71, 76 and 81.

Example 3: Fill in the blanks by following the pattern.

0, 3, 8, 15, 24, ___, ___, ___, ___, ___, ___, ___, ___, ___, ___, ___, ___

Solution: The given numbers are not multiples of any particular whole number; nor is there a fixed difference between them. Therefore, the sequence must be based on a different type of pattern. After considering alternatives, it can be seen that the numbers are $1^2 - 1$, $2^2 - 1$, $3^2 - 1$, and $4^2 - 1$; that is, each number in the sequence is one less than the square of each counting number. Thus, the numbers that complete the sequence are 35, 48, 63, 80, 99, 120, 143, 168, 195, 224, 255, and 288.

Example 4: Fill in the blanks by following the pattern.

6, 14, 24, 36, ___, ___, ___, ___, ___, ___, ___, ___, ___, ___, ___, ___

Solution: The given numbers are not multiples of any particular whole number, nor is there a fixed difference between them. However, there is a pattern formed by the differences between each pair of numbers. Note that the difference between the first two numbers is 8, between the second and third numbers is 10, and between the third and fourth numbers is 12. The difference between each pair increases by 2. Continuing this pattern of differences, the numbers that complete the sequence are 50, 66, 84, 104, 126, 150, 176, 204, 234, 266, 300, and 336.

The *average* of a set of numbers is the sum of the numbers divided by the number of numbers in the set.

Example 5: Find the average of 283, 177, and 302.

Solution: The average of 283, 177, and 302 is their sum divided by 3.

$$\frac{283 + 177 + 302}{3} = 254$$

Thus, the average is 254.

Tables are made up of columns and rows, and are used to display information in a concise, usable form. Data is often listed in columns, with related data listed in subsequent columns according to rows. The problems in this section provide an opportunity to learn how to read a variety of different types of tables.

Example 6: Use the FEDERAL INCOME TAX TABLE on page 122 to find the amount of federal tax for a married couple filing jointly if the taxable income is $40,225.

Solution: Federal income tax is based on the amount of taxable income and the status of the person filing the tax form. The first column (titled "If your taxable income is–") contains the amount of taxable income. Notice that the table on page 122 is for income ranging from $32,000 to $41,000. The income intervals are listed in the first column of each of the three major vertical sections of the table.

To find the tax on $40,225, find the row on the table that corresponds to income that is at least $40,200 but not more than $40,250. This interval contains $40,225. Look across the row to the amount in the column labeled "married, filing jointly." This entry, $6,034, is the tax.

Example 7: Use the STATE INCOME TAX TABLE on page 123 to find the amount of state tax if the taxable income is $38,050.

Solution: Each section of the State Income Tax Table has only two columns, one for the taxable income, and one for the amount of tax. Find the interval on the table that contains $38,050; that is, over $38,010 but not over $38,110. The amount of tax in that row, $1,903, is the state tax.

Example 8: Use the SALES TAX TABLE on page 124 to find the amount of sales tax charged on a sale amounting to $39.95. (Note: The table is compiled for a tax rate of $6\frac{1}{2}$%.)

Solution: Each section of the Sales Tax Table has only two columns, one for the transaction amount (the amount of the purchase), and one for the amount of tax. Find the interval on the table that contains $39.95; that is, the row that is labeled "39.93–40.07." To the right, in the tax column, the tax is stated as "2.60." Thus, the sales tax on $39.95 is $2.60.

The SQUARES AND SQUARE ROOTS TABLE on page 125 lists the square and square root of each number from 1 to 150. If the number is not a perfect square, the square root given is approximate, rounded to three decimal places.

Example 9: Use the SQUARES AND SQUARE ROOTS TABLE on page 125 to find the square of 71.

Solution: Find 71 in the "number" column. The square of 71 is in the same row in the "square" column. Thus, the square of 71 is 5,041.

Example 10: Use the SQUARES AND SQUARE ROOTS TABLE on page 125 to find the approximate square root of 139.

Solution: Find 139 in the "number" column and read the approximate square root in the "square root" column. Thus, the approximate square root of 139 is 11.790.

The SQUARES AND SQUARE ROOTS TABLE can also be used "inside-out" to find square roots of the perfect squares listed in the "square" column.

Example 11: Use the SQUARES AND SQUARE ROOTS TABLE on page 125 to find the square root of 5,929.

Solution: Find 5,929 in the "square" column of the table. Its square root is the number in the "number" column, since that number, when squared, is 5,929. Thus, the square root is 77.

Sequences

Fill in the blanks by following the patterns.

1. 1, 3, 5, 7, __9__, __11__, __13__, __15__, __17__, __19__, __21__, __23__, __25__, __27__, __29__, __31__

2. 2, 4, 6, 8, _____, _____, _____, _____, _____, _____, _____, _____, _____, _____, _____, _____

3. 2, 5, 8, 11, _____, _____, _____, _____, _____, _____, _____, _____, _____, _____, _____, _____

4. 1, 5, 9, 13, _____, _____, _____, _____, _____, _____, _____, _____, _____, _____, _____, _____

5. 10, 20, 30, 40, _____, _____, _____, _____, _____, _____, _____, _____, _____, _____, _____, _____

6. 1, 4, 9, 16, _____, _____, _____, _____, _____, _____, _____, _____, _____, _____, _____, _____

7. 2, 5, 10, 17, _____, _____, _____, _____, _____, _____, _____, _____, _____, _____, _____

8. 1, 3, 6, 10, _____, _____, _____, _____, _____, _____, _____, _____, _____, _____, _____

9. 1, 3, 9, 27, _____, _____, _____, _____, _____, _____, _____, _____, _____, _____

10. 1, 1, 2, 3, 5, 8, _____, _____, _____, _____, _____, _____, _____, _____, _____, _____

Averages

Solve each problem.

---

1. Find the average of 16 and 28. $\dfrac{16 + 28}{2} = 22$

---

2. Find the average of 43 and 67.

---

3. Find the average of 243 and 369.

---

4. Find the average of 392 and 246.

---

5. Find the average of 116, 143, and 161.

---

6. Find the average of 237, 263, and 292.

---

7. Bill's grades for five math quizzes one week were 85, 87, 93, 96, and 84. What was his average for the week?

---

8. Josie is a construction worker. Her income depends on the weather. During the first six months of the year her income was $850, $768, $912, $1,305, $1,420, and $1,801. What was her average monthly income during this time?

---

9. Liam's bowling scores for five games were 159, 126, 148, 189, and 203. What was his average?

---

10. The total rainfall (in inches) for each of the last seven years was 22, 35, 23, 12, 29, 16, and 24. What was the average yearly rainfall for this period?

Sequences

Fill in the blanks by following the patterns.

---

1. 5, 10, 15, 20, __25__, __30__, __35__, __40__, __45__, __50__,

         __55__, __60__, __65__, __70__, __75__, __80__

---

2. 6, 12, 18, 24, _____, _____, _____, _____, _____, _____,

         _____, _____, _____, _____, _____, _____

---

3. 1, 7, 13, 19, _____, _____, _____, _____, _____, _____,

         _____, _____, _____, _____, _____, _____

---

4. 2, 10, 18, 26, _____, _____, _____, _____, _____, _____,

         _____, _____, _____, _____, _____, _____

---

5. 6, 11, 16, 21, _____, _____, _____, _____, _____, _____,

         _____, _____, _____, _____, _____, _____

---

6. 0, 3, 8, 15, _____, _____, _____, _____, _____, _____,

         _____, _____, _____, _____, _____, _____

---

7. 2, 9, 28, 65, _____, _____, _____, _____, _____, _____,

         _____, _____, _____, _____, _____, _____

---

8. 1, 2, 4, 7, _____, _____, _____, _____, _____, _____,

         _____, _____, _____, _____, _____, _____

---

9. 8,192, 4,096, 2,048, 1,024, _____, _____, _____, _____, _____,

         _____, _____, _____, _____, _____

---

10. 1, 4, 3, 8, 5, 16, _____, _____, _____, _____, _____,

         _____, _____, _____, _____, _____

Basic Computation Series 2000: Applying Computational Skills
SECTION 1 Sequences, Averages, and Tables

Averages

Solve each problem.

---

1. Find the average of 27 and 35. $\dfrac{27 + 35}{2} = 31$

---

2. Find the average of 66 and 32.

---

3. Find the average of 267 and 395.

---

4. Find the average of 302 and 526.

---

5. Find the average of 127, 156, and 173.

---

6. Find the average of 244, 256, and 268.

---

7. Linda's grades for five math quizzes one week were 86, 92, 81, 75, and 91. What was her average for the week?

---

8. Pete is a salesman. His income varies from month to month. During the first six months of the year his income was $1,327, $1,867, $1,154, $869, $762, and $963. What was his average monthly income during this time?

---

9. Rosa's bowling scores for five games were 133, 165, 152, 177, and 183. What was her average?

---

10. The total rainfall (in inches) for each of the last seven years was 18, 26, 17, 22, 24, 16, and 17. What was the average yearly rainfall for this period?

Sequences

Fill in the blanks by following the patterns.

1. 3, 6, 9, 12, _15_, _18_, _21_, _24_, _27_, _30_,
_33_, _36_, _39_, _42_, _45_, _48_

2. 9, 18, 27, 36, _____, _____, _____, _____, _____, _____,

_____, _____, _____, _____, _____, _____

3. 3, 11, 19, 27, _____, _____, _____, _____, _____, _____,

_____, _____, _____, _____, _____, _____

4. 5, 9, 13, 17, _____, _____, _____, _____, _____, _____,

_____, _____, _____, _____, _____, _____

5. 8, 18, 28, 38, _____, _____, _____, _____, _____, _____,

_____, _____, _____, _____, _____, _____

6. 1, 2, 4, 8, _____, _____, _____, _____, _____, _____,

_____, _____, _____, _____, _____, _____

7. 2, 3, 5, 9, _____, _____, _____, _____, _____, _____,

_____, _____, _____, _____, _____, _____

8. 1, 4, 8, 13, _____, _____, _____, _____, _____, _____,

_____, _____, _____, _____, _____, _____

9. 1, 2, 5, 10, _____, _____, _____, _____, _____, _____,

_____, _____, _____, _____

10. 1, 3, 2, 4, 3, 5, 4, 6, 5, _____, _____, _____, _____, _____,

_____, _____, _____, _____

Basic Computation Series 2000: Applying Computational Skills
SECTION 1 Sequences, Averages, and Tables

Averages

Solve each problem.

---

1. Find the average of 84 and 60. $\dfrac{84 + 60}{2} = 72$

---

2. Find the average of 43 and 57.

---

3. Find the average of 562 and 434.

---

4. Find the average of 821 and 935.

---

5. Find the average of 132, 184, and 164.

---

6. Find the average of 275, 215, and 233.

---

7. Patty's grades for five math quizzes one week were 76, 89, 83, 90, and 87. What was her average for the week?

---

8. Dimetria operates a beauty shop. Her income for each of the first six months of the year was $927, $833, $1,040, $843, $1,295, and $1,452. What was her average monthly income during this time?

---

9. Larry's bowling scores for 5 games were 117, 152, 136, 147, and 148. What was his average?

---

10. The total rainfall (in inches) for each of the last seven years was 23, 30, 16, 43, 22, 19, and 22. What was the average yearly rainfall for this period?

Basic Computation Series 2000: Applying Computational Skills

Sequences

Fill in the blanks by following the patterns.

1. 8, 16, 24, 32, _40_, _48_, _56_, _64_, _72_, _80_,

    _88_, _96_, _104_, _112_, _120_, _128_

2. 4, 8, 12, 16, _____, _____, _____, _____, _____, _____,

    _____, _____, _____, _____, _____, _____

3. 6, 15, 24, 33, _____, _____, _____, _____, _____, _____,

    _____, _____, _____, _____, _____, _____

4. 3, 12, 21, 30, _____, _____, _____, _____, _____, _____,

    _____, _____, _____, _____, _____, _____

5. 7, 17, 27, 37, _____, _____, _____, _____, _____, _____,

    _____, _____, _____, _____, _____, _____

6. 3, 6, 11, 18, _____, _____, _____, _____, _____, _____,

    _____, _____, _____, _____, _____, _____

7. 1, 8, 27, 64, _____, _____, _____, _____, _____, _____,

    _____, _____, _____, _____, _____, _____

8. 1, 3, 7, 13, _____, _____, _____, _____, _____, _____,

    _____, _____, _____, _____, _____, _____

9. 2, 4, 7, 11, _____, _____, _____, _____, _____, _____,

    _____, _____, _____, _____, _____, _____

10. 2, 5, 4, 10, 6, 15, 8, 20, 10, _____, _____, _____, _____, _____,

    _____, _____, _____, _____, _____

Basic Computation Series 2000: Applying Computational Skills
SECTION 1 Sequences, Averages, and Tables

Averages

Solve each problem.

---

1. Find the average of 38 and 64. $\dfrac{38 + 64}{2} = 51$

---

2. Find the average of 75 and 91.

---

3. Find the average of 516 and 634.

---

4. Find the average of 725 and 927.

---

5. Find the average of 127, 133, and 142.

---

6. Find the average of 285, 290, and 298.

---

7. Nikhil's grades for five math quizzes one week were 99, 85, 64, 72, and 95. What was his average for the week?

---

8. Beth works on commission. Her income for each of the first six months of the year was $982, $695, $1,052, $1,151, $1,214, and $1,320. What was her average monthly income during this time?

---

9. John's bowling scores for 5 games were 182, 170, 144, 131, and 158. What was his average?

---

10. The total rainfall (in inches) for each of the last seven years was 15, 25, 31, 16, 24, 16, and 20. What was the average yearly rainfall for this period?

Sequences

Fill in the blanks by following the patterns.

1. 7, 14, 21, 28, _35_, _42_, _49_, _56_, _63_, _70_,

_77_, _84_, _91_, _98_, _105_, _112_

2. 11, 22, 33, 44, _____, _____, _____, _____, _____, _____,

_____, _____, _____, _____, _____, _____

3. 4, 11, 18, 25, _____, _____, _____, _____, _____, _____,

_____, _____, _____, _____, _____, _____

4. 8, 13, 18, 23, _____, _____, _____, _____, _____, _____,

_____, _____, _____, _____, _____, _____

5. 6, 16, 26, 36, _____, _____, _____, _____, _____, _____,

_____, _____, _____, _____, _____, _____

6. 3, 4, 6, 10, _____, _____, _____, _____, _____, _____,

_____, _____, _____, _____, _____, _____

7. 4, 11, 30, 67, _____, _____, _____, _____, _____, _____,

_____, _____, _____, _____, _____, _____

8. 0, 2, 5, 9, _____, _____, _____, _____, _____, _____,

_____, _____, _____, _____, _____, _____

9. 4, 7, 10, 13, _____, _____, _____, _____, _____, _____,

_____, _____, _____, _____, _____, _____

10. 1, 2, 4, 4, 9, 8, 16, _____, _____, _____, _____, _____, _____,

_____, _____, _____, _____, _____, _____

Basic Computation Series 2000: Applying Computational Skills

Averages

Solve each problem.

1. Find the average of 43 and 67. $\dfrac{43 + 67}{2} = 55$

2. Find the average of 36 and 48.

3. Find the average of 347 and 529.

4. Find the average of 614 and 708.

5. Find the average of 135, 107, and 133.

6. Find the average of 204, 244, and 263.

7. Jim's grades for five math quizzes one week were 88, 82, 87, 83, and 85. What was his average for the week?

8. Antonio's income for each of the first six months of the year was $1,108, $687, $1,202, $1,433, $951, and $1,213. What was his average monthly income during this time?

9. Martha's bowling scores for 5 games were 137, 146, 171, 159, and 182. What was her average?

10. The total rainfall (in inches) for each of the last seven years was 35, 19, 27, 24, 30, 19, and 28. What was the average yearly rainfall for this period?

Reading Tax Tables

Use the tables on pages 122-124 to find the amount of tax on each of the following amounts.

FEDERAL INCOME TAX Married filing jointly		STATE INCOME TAX		SALES TAX	
taxable income	tax	taxable income	tax	amount of purchase	tax
1. $32,578	$4,886	11. $25,700	_____	21. $40.36	_____
2. $36,843	_____	12. $26,090	_____	22. $31.98	_____
3. $34,609	_____	13. $33,190	_____	23. $43.00	_____
4. $37,788	_____	14. $29,850	_____	24. $25.81	_____
5. $33,444	_____	15. $31,275	_____	25. $26.50	_____
6. $39,771	_____	16. $37,295	_____	26. $48.20	_____
7. $40,144	_____	17. $34,960	_____	27. $38.40	_____
8. $35,108	_____	18. $44,830	_____	28. $30.85	_____
9. $38,040	_____	19. $40,000	_____	29. $49.50	_____
10. $39,207	_____	20. $43,666	_____	30. $30.00	_____

Basic Computation Series 2000: Applying Computational Skills
SECTION 1 Sequences, Averages, and Tables

Reading Squares and Square Roots Tables

Use the **SQUARES AND SQUARE ROOTS TABLE** on page 125 to find each number.

Find the square of each number.	Find the approximate square root of each number.	Find the square root of each number.
1. 19 *361*	**11.** 3 _____	**21.** 1,225 _____
2. 62 _____	**12.** 27 _____	**22.** 25 _____
3. 31 _____	**13.** 103 _____	**23.** 5,329 _____
4. 75 _____	**14.** 84 _____	**24.** 625 _____
5. 3 _____	**15.** 23 _____	**25.** 7,921 _____
6. 120 _____	**16.** 95 _____	**26.** 256 _____
7. 136 _____	**17.** 101 _____	**27.** 3,025 _____
8. 85 _____	**18.** 51 _____	**28.** 9,801 _____
9. 150 _____	**19.** 80 _____	**29.** 4,096 _____
10. 45 _____	**20.** 28 _____	**30.** 2,025 _____

Basic Computation Series 2000: Applying Computational Skills
SECTION 1 Sequences, Averages, and Tables

Reading Tax Tables

Use the tables on pages 122-124 to find the amount of tax on each of the following amounts.

FEDERAL INCOME TAX Married filing jointly		STATE INCOME TAX		SALES TAX	
taxable income	tax	taxable income	tax	amount of purchase	tax
1. $33,120	$4,969	**11.** $26,681	_____	**21.** $37.70	_____
2. $39,551	_____	**12.** $30,300	_____	**22.** $26.70	_____
3. $35,875	_____	**13.** $32,899	_____	**23.** $39.50	_____
4. $34,316	_____	**14.** $41,185	_____	**24.** $49.20	_____
5. $37,941	_____	**15.** $49,421	_____	**25.** $32.67	_____
6. $32,230	_____	**16.** $45,327	_____	**26.** $47.20	_____
7. $40,648	_____	**17.** $34,229	_____	**27.** $41.84	_____
8. $36,842	_____	**18.** $27,400	_____	**28.** $28.12	_____
9. $38,669	_____	**19.** $42,890	_____	**29.** $25.39	_____
10. $35,125	_____	**20.** $33,800	_____	**30.** $33.85	_____

Reading Squares and Square Roots Tables

Use the SQUARES AND SQUARE ROOTS TABLE on page 125 to find each number.

Find the square of each number.	Find the approximate square root of each number.	Find the square root of each number.
1. 50 2,500	**11.** 54 _____	**21.** 3,249 _____
2. 7 _____	**12.** 75 _____	**22.** 289 _____
3. 91 _____	**13.** 5 _____	**23.** 2,209 _____
4. 65 _____	**14.** 46 _____	**24.** 5,625 _____
5. 123 _____	**15.** 120 _____	**25.** 8,281 _____
6. 78 _____	**16.** 114 _____	**26.** 49 _____
7. 20 _____	**17.** 27 _____	**27.** 11,664 _____
8. 140 _____	**18.** 87 _____	**28.** 5,776 _____
9. 116 _____	**19.** 63 _____	**29.** 729 _____
10. 34 _____	**20.** 109 _____	**30.** 1,369 _____

Reading Tax Tables

Use the tables on pages 122-124 to find the amount of tax on each of the following amounts.

FEDERAL INCOME TAX Married filing jointly		STATE INCOME TAX		SALES TAX	
taxable income	tax	taxable income	tax	amount of purchase	tax
1. $40,410	$6,064	11. $48,672	_____	21. $38.80	_____
2. $32,742	_____	12. $39,400	_____	22. $34.50	_____
3. $34,700	_____	13. $40,802	_____	23. $29.40	_____
4. $37,232	_____	14. $32,434	_____	24. $43.55	_____
5. $39,876	_____	15. $29,868	_____	25. $41.85	_____
6. $36,988	_____	16. $31,000	_____	26. $25.50	_____
7. $38,690	_____	17. $42,960	_____	27. $27.63	_____
8. $33,305	_____	18. $30,420	_____	28. $50.25	_____
9. $35,958	_____	19. $33,467	_____	29. $30.60	_____
10. $40,980	_____	20. $38,276	_____	30. $45.80	_____

Reading Squares and Square Roots Tables

Use the **SQUARES AND SQUARE ROOTS TABLE** on page 125 to find each number.

Find the square of each number.		Find the approximate square root of each number.		Find the square root of each number.	
1. 124	_15,376_	**11.** 71	_____	**21.** 841	_____
2. 23	_____	**12.** 125	_____	**22.** 81	_____
3. 142	_____	**13.** 7	_____	**23.** 10,816	_____
4. 38	_____	**14.** 150	_____	**24.** 1,521	_____
5. 108	_____	**15.** 92	_____	**25.** 8,649	_____
6. 81	_____	**16.** 30	_____	**26.** 361	_____
7. 10	_____	**17.** 140	_____	**27.** 12,100	_____
8. 53	_____	**18.** 80	_____	**28.** 3,481	_____
9. 103	_____	**19.** 116	_____	**29.** 11,236	_____
10. 68	_____	**20.** 85	_____	**30.** 2,401	_____

Reading Tax Tables

Use the tables on pages 122-124 to find the amount of tax on each of the following amounts.

FEDERAL INCOME TAX Married filing jointly	STATE INCOME TAX	SALES TAX
taxable income tax	taxable income tax	amount of purchase tax
1. $32,807 $4,924	**11.** $30,885 _____	**21.** $28.35 _____
2. $40,002 _____	**12.** $29,975 _____	**22.** $31.80 _____
3. $35,041 _____	**13.** $41,392 _____	**23.** $26.95 _____
4. $33,727 _____	**14.** $40,500 _____	**24.** $40.36 _____
5. $39,350 _____	**15.** $32,461 _____	**25.** $36.35 _____
6. $34,456 _____	**16.** $47,100 _____	**26.** $33.80 _____
7. $38,930 _____	**17.** $43,100 _____	**27.** $48.81 _____
8. $36,702 _____	**18.** $29,525 _____	**28.** $46.35 _____
9. $40,923 _____	**19.** $44,380 _____	**29.** $44.71 _____
10. $37,385 _____	**20.** $31,690 _____	**30.** $29.50 _____

Reading Squares and Square Roots Tables

Use the **SQUARES AND SQUARE ROOTS TABLE** on page 125 to find each number.

Find the square of each number.	Find the approximate square root of each number.	Find the square root of each number.
1. 70 _4,900_	**11.** 35 _____	**21.** 1,681 _____
2. 13 _____	**12.** 85 _____	**22.** 441 _____
3. 112 _____	**13.** 8 _____	**23.** 10,404 _____
4. 57 _____	**14.** 133 _____	**24.** 2,601 _____
5. 130 _____	**15.** 62 _____	**25.** 12,544 _____
6. 25 _____	**16.** 73 _____	**26.** 961 _____
7. 108 _____	**17.** 114 _____	**27.** 3,721 _____
8. 82 _____	**18.** 54 _____	**28.** 121 _____
9. 76 _____	**19.** 126 _____	**29.** 9,025 _____
10. 40 _____	**20.** 12 _____	**30.** 4,356 _____

Reading Tax Tables

Use the tables on pages 122-124 to find the amount of tax on each of the following amounts.

FEDERAL INCOME TAX Married filing jointly	STATE INCOME TAX	SALES TAX
taxable income tax	taxable income tax	amount of purchase tax
1. $33,792 $5,066	**11.** $42,590 _____	**21.** $47.82 _____
2. $34,843 _____	**12.** $42,206 _____	**22.** $34.85 _____
3. $39,108 _____	**13.** $39,600 _____	**23.** $29.38 _____
4. $37,119 _____	**14.** $33,785 _____	**24.** $44.20 _____
5. $35,395 _____	**15.** $31,467 _____	**25.** $31.36 _____
6. $32,558 _____	**16.** $30,075 _____	**26.** $27.60 _____
7. $38,985 _____	**17.** $26,807 _____	**27.** $37.80 _____
8. $37,186 _____	**18.** $49,590 _____	**28.** $41.40 _____
9. $36,460 _____	**19.** $31,000 _____	**29.** $49.90 _____
10. $39,800 _____	**20.** $43,208 _____	**30.** $33.35 _____

Reading Squares and Square Roots Tables

Use the SQUARES AND SQUARE ROOTS TABLE on page 125 to find each number.

Find the square of each number.	Find the approximate square root of each number.	Find the square root of each number.
1. 125 _15,625_	**11.** 96 _____	**21.** 1,089 _____
2. 29 _____	**12.** 46 _____	**22.** 9,409 _____
3. 98 _____	**13.** 103 _____	**23.** 1,849 _____
4. 74 _____	**14.** 148 _____	**24.** 13,456 _____
5. 115 _____	**15.** 17 _____	**25.** 196 _____
6. 16 _____	**16.** 133 _____	**26.** 3,844 _____
7. 132 _____	**17.** 82 _____	**27.** 10,000 _____
8. 43 _____	**18.** 67 _____	**28.** 529 _____
9. 135 _____	**19.** 55 _____	**29.** 900 _____
10. 60 _____	**20.** 19 _____	**30.** 2,809 _____

Basic Computation Series 2000: Applying Computational Skills
SECTION 1 Sequences, Averages, and Tables

Graphs and Maps

Graphs and maps provide "pictures" of information in useful formats. Three types of graphs are bar graphs, line graphs, and circle graphs. An example of each is shown below.

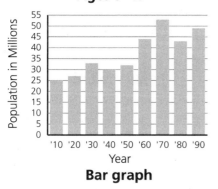

U.S. School Population Ages 5–17

Bar graph

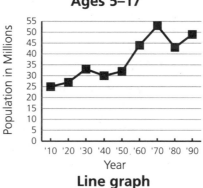

U.S. School Population Ages 5–17

Line graph

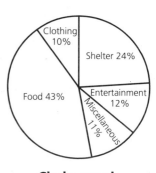

Family Budget

Circle graph

The bar graph and the line graph pictured above both illustrate the same data, the U.S. school population, ages 5–17, for the years 1910–1990. Each graph contains an x-axis (the horizontal axis) and a y-axis (the vertical axis). The years are marked on the x-axis, and the population is marked on the y-axis. The circle graph shows how one family has planned its budget. Each section of the circle represents a certain percent of the total budget. The size of each section is determined by the percent.

Example 1: Use the bar graph shown to approximate the net farm income in Oklahoma in 1972 and 1973.

Solution: Find the bar that represents 1972. The top of the bar is just below the horizontal line that indicates an income of $4,000. Thus, the income is approximately $3,900.

In a similar manner, the top of the bar that represents 1973 is a little more than half-way between $7,000 and $8,000. Thus, the income is approximately $7,600.

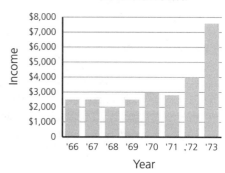

Net Farm Income in Oklahoma

Example 2: Use the line graph shown to approximate the speed at which an elk and a human can run.

Solution: Find "Elk" on the *x*-axis, and locate the square on the graph directly above "Elk." This square marks the speed of the elk. The center of the square is about three-fourths of the way between 40 and 50. Thus, the speed is approximately 47 mph.

Find "Human" on the *x*-axis and locate the square on the graph directly above "Human." This square marks the speed of a human. The center of the square is about three-fourths of the way between 20 and 30. Thus, the speed is approximately 27 mph.

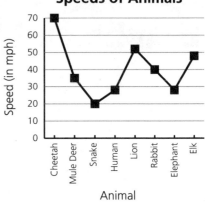

Speeds of Animals

Example 3: Use the given information to construct a bar graph of the population of the given U.S. Cities in 1990 on the outline provided.

State	Population
New York, NY	7,322,654
Los Angeles, CA	3,485,557
Chicago, IL	2,783,726
Houston, TX	1,629,902
Philadelphia, PA	1,585,577
San Diego, CA	1,110,623

Solution: Since the population of New York City is about 7.3 million, find the point on the *y*-axis that would approximate that number. Mark the top of the bar for New York City level with this point, and draw the bar. In a similar way, find points on the *y*-axis that approximate the population of each of the other cities and draw bars for them. Shade the bars so as to differentiate between the bars and the blank areas of the graph.

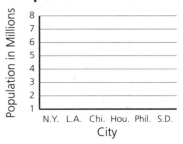

Population of U.S. Cities

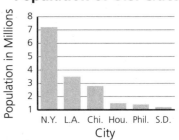

Population of U.S. Cities

Example 4: Use the given information concerning state sales tax to construct a line graph on the outline provided.

State	Tax Rate
Alabama	4.0%
Hawaii	4.0%
Kansas	6.9%
Maryland	5.0%
Minnesota	6.5%
Oklahoma	4.5%

Solution: Since the state sales tax in Alabama is 4.0%, locate the point on the *y*-axis that represents 4.0%. Plot a point directly above "AL" on the *x*-axis, level with the 4.0% point on the *y*-axis. This is the point on the graph that represents the state sales tax in Alabama. In a similar way, locate and mark the points that represent the sales tax in each of the other states and join the points to form the graph.

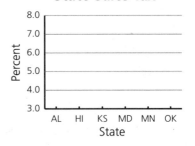

State Sales Tax

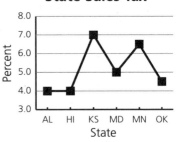

State Sales Tax

Example 5: Use the circle graph shown to determine the approximate number of luxury automobiles sold in the United States in 1996 out of a total of 133,599,578 vehicles sold.

Passenger Automobiles (By Size)

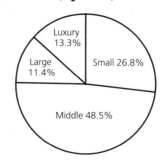

Solution: The graph shows that 13.3% of the automobiles sold were luxury cars. The number of luxury automobiles sold is 13.3% of 133,599,578. Since 13.3% of 133,599,578 is approximately 17,768,744, the number of luxury cars sold in 1996 was approximately 17,768,744.

Example 6: Use the given information to make a circle graph showing the percent of enlisted women in the branches of the armed forces.

Branch of Service	Number of Women
Women's Army Corps	35,656
Air Force	16,500
Women's Marines	2,767
Coast Guard	420
Navy	15,114

Women in the Armed Forces

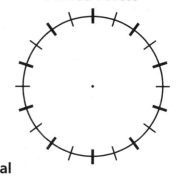

Solution: The total number of women is 70,457. Find the percent of the total number of women in each branch. Use the percents to determine the portion of the circle that will represent each branch of service. (Round percents to the nearest whole number.)

Branch of Service	Number of Women	Percent of Total
Women's Army Corps	35,656	$\frac{35,656}{70,457} \approx 51\%$
Air Force	16,500	$\frac{16,500}{70,457} \approx 23\%$
Women's Marines	2,767	$\frac{2,767}{70,457} \approx 4\%$
Coast Guard	420	$\frac{420}{70,457} \approx 1\%$
Navy	15,114	$\frac{15,114}{70,457} \approx 21\%$

Notice that there are 20 marks on the circle. If lines were drawn connecting each of these marks to the center of the circle, each section formed would represent 5% of the circle. To construct a section that will represent 51% (the percent of enlisted women that are in the Women's Army Corps), mark off and label an area that contains slightly more than 10 of the sections. From the edge of this section, construct an area representing 23% (the percent of enlisted women that are in the Air Force) by marking off and labeling an area containing about $4\frac{1}{2}$ of the sections. For the section that needs to be 4% of the circle (Women's Marines), mark off and label an area that is slightly smaller than one 5% section. For the section that is to represent the Navy (21%), mark off and label a section that contains a bit more than 4 sections. Label the tiny sliver left over as the section that represents women in the Coast Guard (1%). (Note: A protractor and/or a compass may prove helpful in constructing circle graphs.)

Women in the Armed Forces

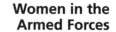
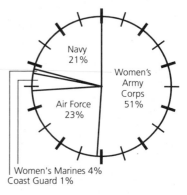

Because of its usefulness in everyday life, map reading is an important skill to develop. Many maps include a table that shows distances between certain cities. To find distances between cities that are not listed in the table, the scale to which the map has been drawn is given. This scale provides a ratio that shows the relationship between distances on the map and actual distances. An approximation of the distance between any two locations can be found by using a ruler to measure the distance on the map and using the scale to convert the measured distance to the actual distance.

The map-reading problems in this section of the book can be solved using the Map of Lincoln County provided on page 126. The scale of the map indicates that 10 mm = 25 km. To find the distance between any two locations, measure the distance on the map using a ruler marked in millimeters, and write a proportion using the scale of the map. Solve the proportion by setting the cross products equal to each other and finding the missing value. This value will be an approximation of the actual distance between the locations. Study the examples below to see how this is done.

Example 7: Using the map of Lincoln County on page 126, find the approximate distance in kilometers from town A to town B.

Solution: Measuring from the center of the dot at A to the center of the dot at B, the map distance is found to be 20 mm. The scale of the map indicates that 10 mm = 25 km. If x represents the actual distance from town A to town B, the following proportion can be written:

$$\frac{10}{25} = \frac{20}{x}$$

Cross multiply, and solve the resulting equation.

$$10x = 500$$
$$x = 50$$

Thus, the approximate distance from town A to town B is 50 km.

Example 8: Using the same map, find the approximate distance, correct to the nearest tenth kilometer, from town T to town KK.

Solution: Measuring from the center of the dot at T to the center of the dot at KK, the map distance is found to be 57 mm. The scale of the map indicates that 10 mm = 25 km. If x represents the actual distance from town T to town KK, the following proportion can be written:

$$\frac{10}{25} = \frac{57}{x}$$

Cross multiply, and solve the resulting equation.

$$10x = 1{,}425$$
$$x = 142.5$$

Thus, the approximate distance from town T to town KK is 142.5 km.

Reading Bar Graphs

Use the bar graphs to approximate each answer.

1. What was the price per gallon of gasoline for each year?

a. 1975 ___$0.57___

b. 1980 _____

c. 1985 _____

d. 1990 _____

e. 1991 _____

f. 1993 _____

g. 1995 _____

h. 1996 _____

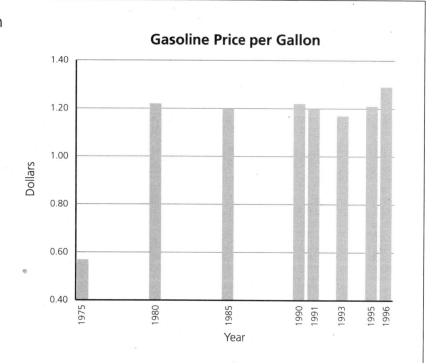

Gasoline Price per Gallon

2. What was the consumer price index for each year?

a. 1985 _____

b. 1986 _____

c. 1987 _____

d. 1988 _____

e. 1989 _____

f. 1990 _____

g. 1991 _____

h. 1992 _____

i. 1993 _____

j. 1994 _____

k. 1995 _____

l. 1996 _____

Consumer Price Index

Reading Line Graphs

Use the line graphs to approximate each answer.

1. What was the prime interest rate for each month?

a. March _____6.2%_____

b. April _____

c. May _____

d. June _____

e. July _____

f. August _____

g. September _____

h. October _____

i. November _____

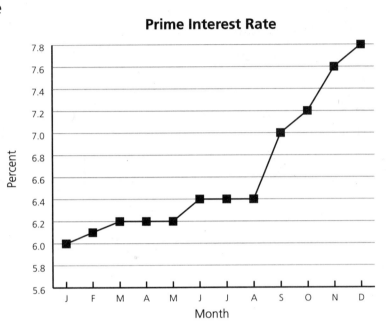

Prime Interest Rate

2. What was the Federal Reserve discount rate for each year?

a. 1982 _____

b. 1983 _____

c. 1984 _____

d. 1985 _____

e. 1986 _____

f. 1987 _____

g. 1988 _____

h. 1989 _____

i. 1990 _____

j. 1991 _____

k. 1992 _____

l. 1993 _____

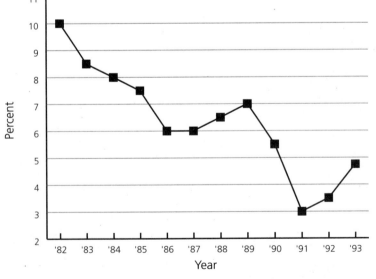

Federal Reserve Discount Rate

Reading Bar Graphs

Use the bar graphs to approximate each answer.

1. What is the average rainfall in Georgia for each month?

   a. January _____ 4 in. _____

   b. February _____

   c. March _____

   d. April _____

   e. May _____

   f. June _____

   g. July _____

   h. August _____

   i. September _____

   j. October _____

   k. November _____

   l. December _____

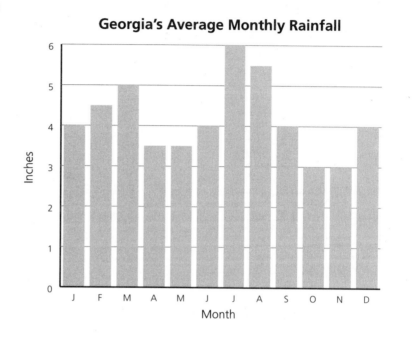

Georgia's Average Monthly Rainfall

2. What is the average rainfall in Ohio for each month?

   a. January _____

   b. February _____

   c. March _____

   d. April _____

   e. May _____

   f. June _____

   g. July _____

   h. August _____

   i. September _____

   j. October _____

   k. November _____

   l. December _____

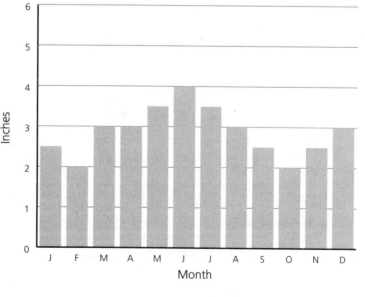

Ohio's Average Monthly Rainfall

Basic Computation Series 2000: Applying Computational Skills
SECTION 2 Graphs and Maps

Reading Line Graphs

Use the line graphs to approximate each answer.

1. What is the average temperature in Oklahoma for each month?

   a. January ___40°F___

   b. February _____

   c. March _____

   d. April _____

   e. May _____

   f. June _____

   g. July _____

   h. August _____

   i. September _____

   j. October _____

   k. November _____

   l. December _____

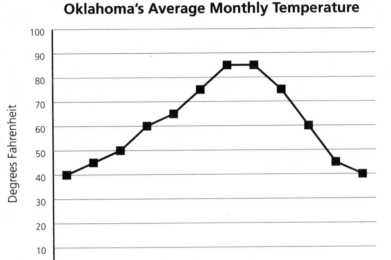

Oklahoma's Average Monthly Temperature

2. What is the average temperature in California for each month?

   a. January _____

   b. February _____

   c. March _____

   d. April _____

   e. May _____

   f. June _____

   g. July _____

   h. August _____

   i. September _____

   j. October _____

   k. November _____

   l. December _____

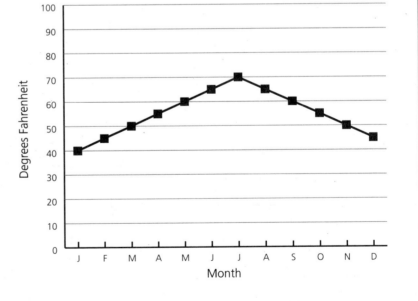

California's Average Monthly Temperature

Basic Computation Series 2000: Applying Computational Skills

Reading Bar Graphs

Use the bar graphs to approximate each answer.

1. What percent of the voters voted each year?

   a. 1930 _____35%_____

   b. 1934 _____

   c. 1938 _____

   d. 1942 _____

   e. 1946 _____

   f. 1950 _____

   g. 1954 _____

   h. 1958 _____

   i. 1962 _____

   j. 1966 _____

   k. 1970 _____

   l. 1974 _____

   m. 1978 _____

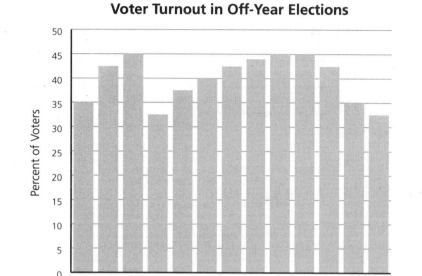

Voter Turnout in Off-Year Elections

2. What percent of the labor force was unemployed during each month?

   a. January _____

   b. February _____

   c. March _____

   d. April _____

   e. May _____

   f. June _____

   g. July _____

   h. August _____

   i. September _____

   j. October _____

   k. November _____

   l. December _____

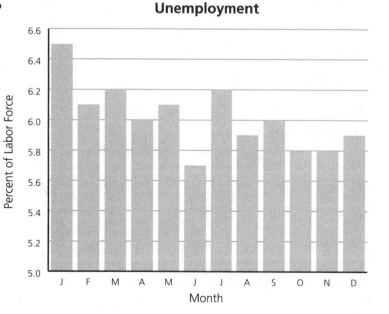

Unemployment

Reading Line Graphs

Use the line graphs to approximate each answer.

1. How many passenger cars were sold in the U.S. each year?

   a. 1960 *6.7 million*

   b. 1965 _____

   c. 1970 _____

   d. 1975 _____

   e. 1980 _____

   f. 1985 _____

   g. 1990 _____

   h. 1995 _____

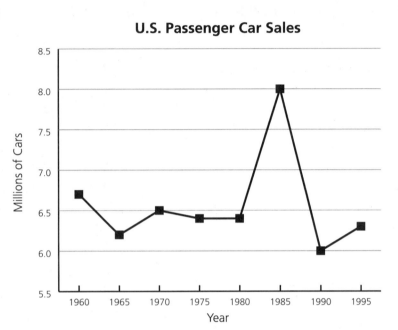

U.S. Passenger Car Sales

2. What was the population in each part of the United States when this graph was constructed?

   a. New England _____

   b. Middle Atlantic _____

   c. East North Central _____

   d. West North Central _____

   e. South Atlantic _____

   f. East South Central _____

   g. West South Central _____

   h. Mountain _____

   i. Pacific _____

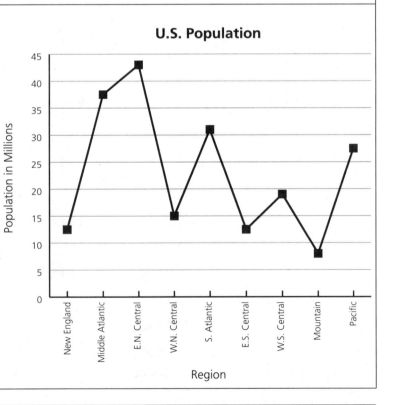

U.S. Population

Reading Bar Graphs

Use the bar graphs to approximate each answer.

1. What were the deposits in savings and loan associations each month?

   a. May _$393 billion_

   b. June _____

   c. July _____

   d. August _____

   e. September _____

   f. October _____

   g. November _____

   h. December _____

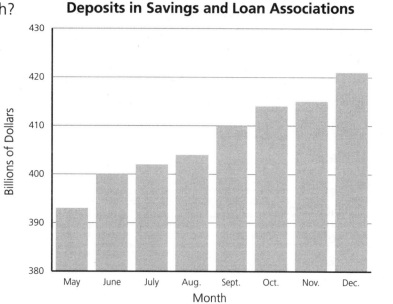

Deposits in Savings and Loan Associations

2. What was the number of housing units started each year?

   a. 1970 _____

   b. 1971 _____

   c. 1972 _____

   d. 1973 _____

   e. 1974 _____

   f. 1975 _____

   g. 1976 _____

   h. 1977 _____

   i. 1978 _____

   j. 1979 _____

   k. 1980 _____

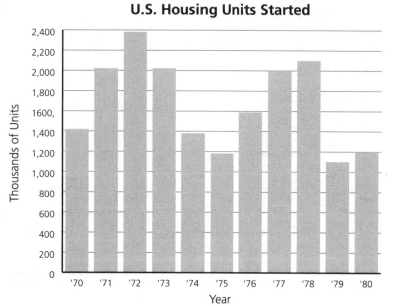

U.S. Housing Units Started

Reading Line Graphs

Use the line graphs to approximate each answer.

1. To the nearest ten-thousand, what were the TV advertising expenditures for the following companies?

  a. GM $\underline{\$1,060,000}$

  b. P&G _____

  c. Chrysler _____

  d. Pepsico _____

  e. Disney _____

  f. McDonald's _____

  g. Sony _____

  h. Kellogg's _____

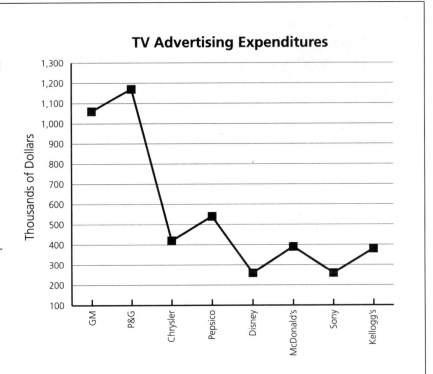

TV Advertising Expenditures

2. How many cars were produced in the United States each year?

  a. 1990 _____

  b. 1991 _____

  c. 1992 _____

  d. 1993 _____

  e. 1994 _____

  f. 1995 _____

  g. 1996 _____

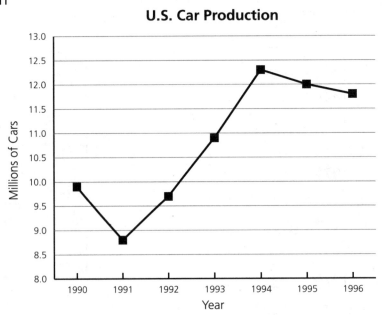

U.S. Car Production

Basic Computation Series 2000: Applying Computational Skills

Reading Bar Graphs

Use the bar graphs to approximate each answer.

1. What was the U.S. school population, ages 5–17, each year?

  a. 1910 <u>25 million</u>

  b. 1920 _____

  c. 1930 _____

  d. 1940 _____

  e. 1950 _____

  f. 1960 _____

  g. 1970 _____

  h. 1980 _____

  i. 1990 _____

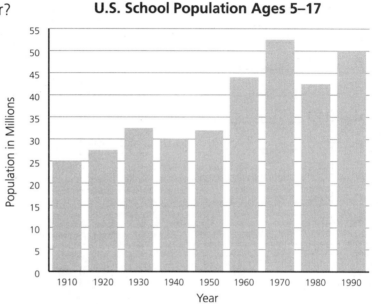

U.S. School Population Ages 5–17

2. What was the average daily attendance in U.S. public schools each year?

  a. 1910 _____

  b. 1920 _____

  c. 1930 _____

  d. 1940 _____

  e. 1950 _____

  f. 1960 _____

  g. 1970 _____

  h. 1980 _____

  i. 1990 _____

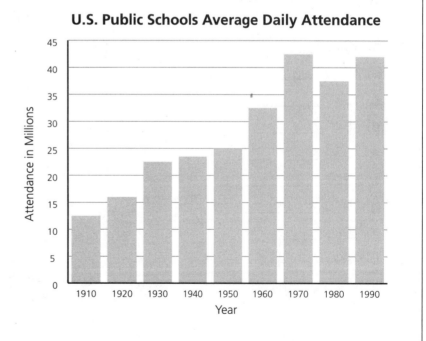

U.S. Public Schools Average Daily Attendance

Reading Line Graphs

Use the line graphs to approximate each answer.

1. What was the number of teachers in U.S. public schools each year?

a. 1910 __500,000__

b. 1920 _____

c. 1930 _____

d. 1940 _____

e. 1950 _____

f. 1960 _____

g. 1970 _____

h. 1980 _____

i. 1990 _____

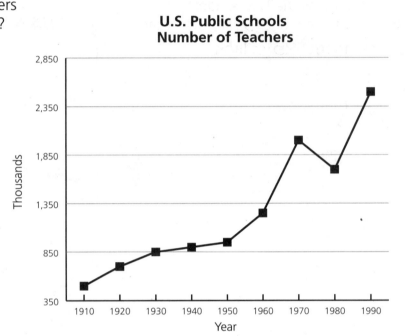

**U.S. Public Schools
Number of Teachers**

2. What was the average annual salary of U.S. teachers each year?

a. 1910 _____

b. 1920 _____

c. 1930 _____

d. 1940 _____

e. 1950 _____

f. 1960 _____

g. 1970 _____

h. 1980 _____

i. 1990 _____

Average Annual Salary of U.S. Teachers

Basic Computation Series 2000: Applying Computational Skills

Constructing Bar Graphs

Use the given information to construct each bar graph.

1. Construct a bar graph showing the percent change in the consumer price index for each quarter of each year listed.

quarter

	1st	2nd	3rd	4th
1993	9%	7.8%	5%	5.9%
1994	9%	10.4%	8.8%	8.8%
1995	13.1%	13.1%	13.8%	13.8%
1996	11.5%	11.5%	7.2%	12.8%

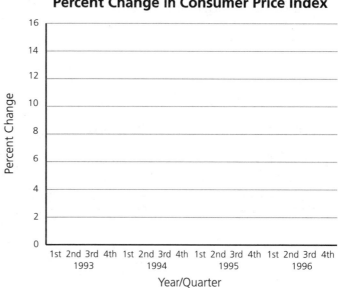

2. Construct a bar graph showing the average prime interest rate for January through December.

Jan.	10%	July	10%
Feb.	10%	Aug	11%
Mar.	10%	Sept.	11%
Apr.	8%	Oct.	9%
May	9%	Nov.	8%
June	7%	Dec.	9%

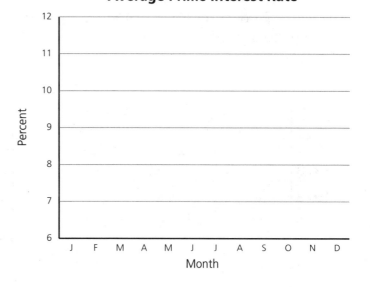

Constructing Line Graphs

Use the given information to construct each line graph.

1. Construct a line graph showing the rate of unemployment for each quarter of each year listed.

quarter

	1st	2nd	3rd	4th
1993	7.5%	7.1%	6.8%	6.5%
1994	6.2%	6%	6%	5.8%
1995	5.7%	5.8%	5.8%	5.9%
1996	6.1%	7.2%	7.5%	8%

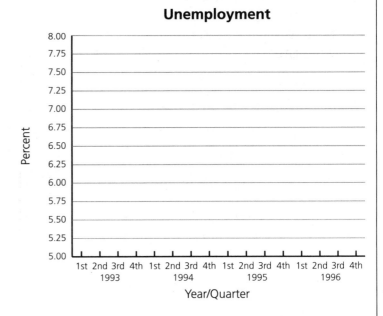

2. Construct a line graph showing the percent change in the Gross National Product for each quarter of the years listed.

quarter

	1st	2nd	3rd	4th
1977	8.8%	4.8%	7%	2.1%
1978	1.8%	8.1%	2.9%	5.7%
1979	1%	−2.3%	3%	2%
1980	1.1%	−9.6%	0.9%	2%

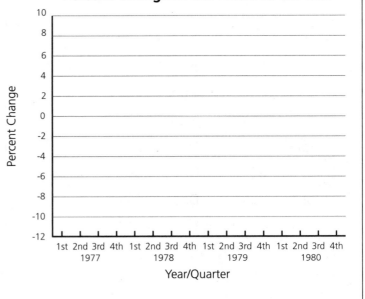

Constructing Bar Graphs

Use the given information to construct each bar graph.

1. Construct a bar graph showing the net sales for a certain company.

1992: $2,300,000,000

1993: $2,600,000,000

1994: $3,400,000,000

1995: $3,600,000,000

1996: $4,300,000,000

1997: $3,800,000,000

1998: $3,200,000,000

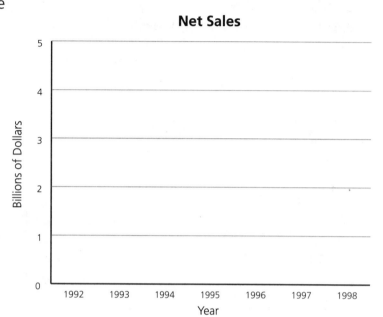

Net Sales

2. Construct a bar graph showing the net profit for a certain company.

1992: $102,000,000

1993: $134,000,000

1994: $190,000,000

1995: $150,000,000

1996: $185,000,000

1997: $140,000,000

1998: $170,000,000

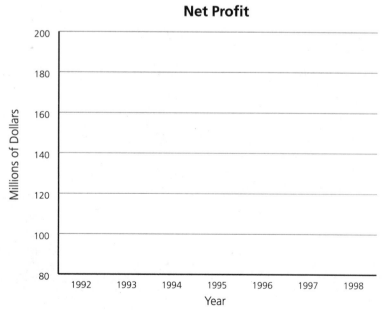

Net Profit

Constructing Line Graphs

Use the given information to construct a line graph.

Construct a line graph showing the average amount of daylight each month. (Data given for the 15th day of the month, 40° north latitude, Greenwich Mean Time)

	Sunrise (A.M.)	Sunset (P.M.)
January	7:20	4:58
February	6:55	5:35
March	6:12	6:07
April	5:22	6:38
May	4:45	7:08
June	4:30	7:30
July	4:44	7:28
August	5:11	6:57
September	5:41	6:08
October	6:10	5:21
November	6:45	4:44
December	7:15	4:36

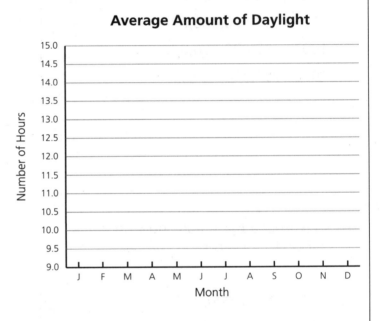

Average Amount of Daylight

Constructing Bar Graphs

Use the given information to construct each bar graph.

1. Construct a bar graph showing the leading causes of death in persons under 65 years of age.

Disease of heart and blood vessels	260,000
Cancer	140,000
Accidents	85,000
Pneumonia and influenza	30,000
Diabetes	10,000
All other causes	205,000

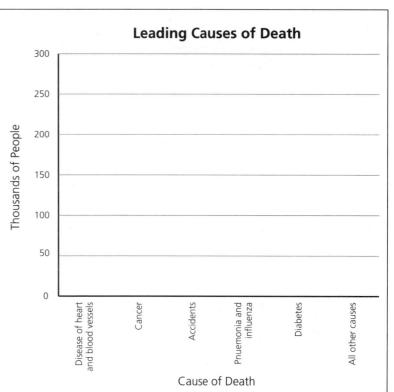

Leading Causes of Death

2. Construct a bar graph showing the life expectancy at birth of a U.S. male, according to birth year.

1910:	46.3
1920:	53.6
1930:	58.1
1940:	60.8
1950:	65.6
1960:	66.6
1970:	67.1
1980:	68.6
1990:	71.8

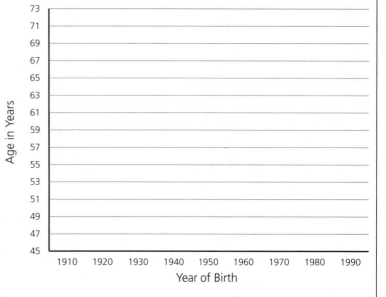

Male Life Expectancy at Birth

Basic Computation Series 2000: Applying Computational Skills

Constructing Line Graphs

Use the given information to construct each line graph.

1. Construct a line graph showing the life expectancy at birth of a U.S. female, according to birth year.

Year	Age
1910:	48.3
1920:	54.6
1930:	61.6
1940:	65.2
1950:	71.1
1960:	73.1
1970:	74.6
1980:	76.1
1990:	78.8

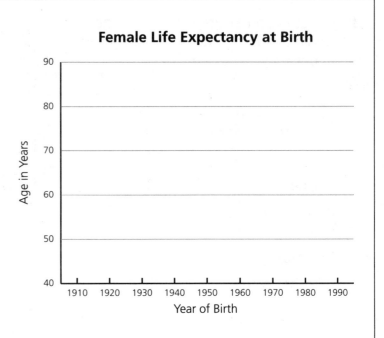

2. Construct a line graph showing the number of births in the United States for each year.

Year	Births
1975:	3,144,000
1980:	3,612,000
1985:	3,761,000
1990:	4,158,000
1995:	3,892,000

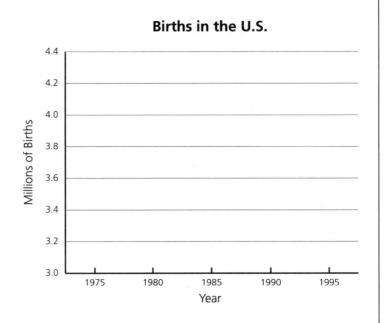

Constructing Bar Graphs

Use the given information to construct a bar graph.

Construct a bar graph showing the annual income in both 1990 and 1996 for the occupations listed. Shade the 1990 portion of the graph. The numbers before each occupation have been used to label the bars. The first bar has been drawn and shaded.

Occupation		1990	1996
1)	Social Security recipient	$ 3,901	$ 5,504
2)	Steelworker	28,076	32,541
3)	Autoworker	30,128	35,912
4)	Petrochemical worker	31,028	34,002
5)	Truck driver	18,319	34,602
6)	U.S. Army major	18,121	33,212
7)	Plumber	26,140	31,020
8)	Policeman	27,516	36,745
9)	Federal civil servant GS7	29,110	38,841
10)	Computer programmer	34,026	46,640
11)	Engineer	41,319	56,446
12)	Corporate lawyer	65,122	91,640
13)	Accountant	24,510	39,825
14)	U.S. senator	75,000	90,000
15)	Librarian	23,840	29,076
16)	Welfare recipient	4,119	6,814

Annual Income

Income in Thousands of Dollars

Occupation

Basic Computation Series 2000: Applying Computational Skills
SECTION 2 Graphs and Maps

Constructing Line Graphs

Use the given information to construct each line graph.

1. Construct a line graph showing the Smith's expenses for gas and electricity last year.

Jan.	$55.10	July	$53.78
Feb.	$49.86	Aug	$37.12
Mar.	$79.30	Sept.	$35.22
Apr.	$58.66	Oct.	$43.15
May	$61.91	Nov.	$42.58
June	$40.64	Dec.	$66.23

Gas and Electricity Expenses

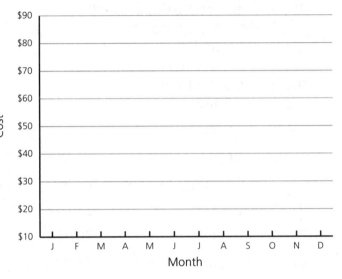

2. Construct a line graph showing both the birthrate and death rate per 1,000 population in the countries listed. Show the birthrate as a solid line and the death rate as a dashed line.

Country	Birthrate	Death Rate
France	14	10
India	34	14
Israel	28	7
Japan	16	6
Mexico	31	6
United States	15	9
United Kingdom	12	12

Birthrate/Death Rate per 1,000 Population

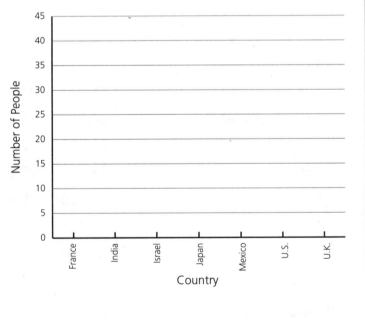

Constructing Bar Graphs

Use the given information to construct each bar graph.

1. The grades for 24 students are listed below. Tally the number of students receiving each letter grade and construct a bar graph showing the grade distribution in the class.

1. B	9. C	17. C
2. C	10. D	18. A
3. A	11. B	19. C
4. C	12. C	20. B
5. D	13. C	21. C
6. D	14. C	22. C
7. B	15. F	23. D
8. C	16. B	24. C

Grade Distribution

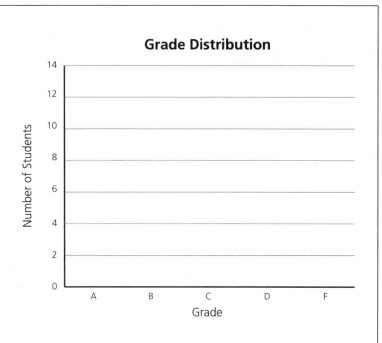

2. Construct a bar graph showing the average annual job openings for 1985-1996.

Job	No. of Openings
1. Bookkeepers	95,000
2. Carpenters	67,000
3. Computer programmers	9,700
4. Cooks and chefs	79,000
5. Cosmetologists	30,000
6. Dental assistants	13,500
7. Firefighters	8,200
8. Mathematicians	1,000
9. Musicians	7,200
10. Keyboard operators	63,000

Average Annual Job Openings

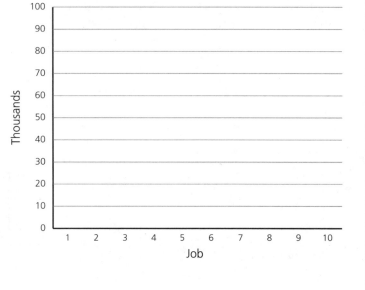

Constructing Line Graphs

Use the given information to construct each line graph.

1. Nancy had the following test scores for one quarter. Construct a line graph showing her test performance.

Test No.	Grade	Test No.	Grade
1	92	6	95
2	85	7	82
3	100	8	71
4	78	9	88
5	81		

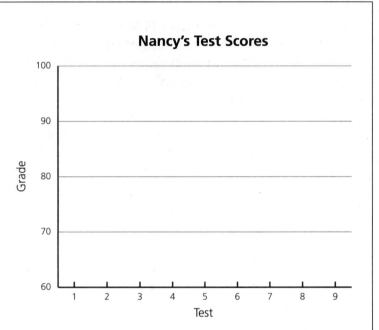

Nancy's Test Scores

2. The hourly temperatures in a city on a winter day are listed below. Construct a line graph showing the temperature (in degrees Fahrenheit) each hour.

Time	Temp.	Time	Temp.
6 A.M.	10°	1 P.M.	30°
7 A.M.	8°	2 P.M.	45°
8 A.M.	15°	3 P.M.	60°
9 A.M.	18°	4 P.M.	51°
10 A.M.	19°	5 P.M.	50°
11 A.M.	20°	6 P.M.	47°
12 Noon	25°		

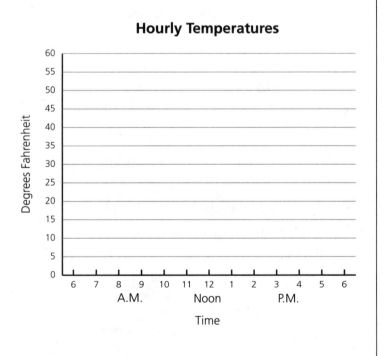

Hourly Temperatures

Reading Circle Graphs

Use the circle graphs to find each answer.

1. The circle graph shows what products account for each dollar in sales at the Good Food Store. Total sales for one month were $75,000. What was the amount of sales in each category?

a. groceries ___$22,500___

b. meat _____

c. produce _____

d. bakery _____

e. dairy _____

f. sundries _____

g. beverages _____

h. other _____

Sales

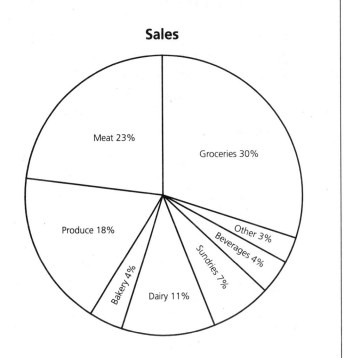

2. The circle graph shows how each dollar of manufacturing overhead is spent at Gloom Manufacturing. Total expenditures were $44,400. How much was spent in each category?

a. labor _____

b. heat and power _____

c. repairs _____

d. depreciation _____

e. insurance _____

f. property taxes _____

g. supplies _____

h. miscellaneous _____

Expenditures

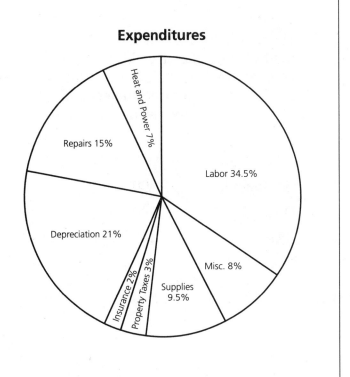

Constructing Circle Graphs

Use the given information to construct each circle graph. The heavy marks on the circle divide the circle into 10 equal parts (10% of the circle). The lighter marks are halfway between the heavy marks. Round values to the nearest percent.

1. Construct a circle graph showing the percentage of world wheat and coarse grain production for each geographic region. The production is given in millions of tons.

Far East	196
Near East	42
Africa	47
USSR	205
Oceania	19
Latin America	68
North America	290
Western Europe	144
Eastern Europe	77

Wheat and Coarse Grain Production

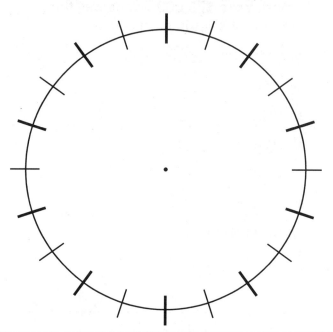

2. The points for the semester in the mathematics class that Miss Selany teaches are listed below. Construct a circle graph showing the portion of the grade determined by each factor.

Citizenship	90 points
Homework	90 points
Quizzes	180 points
Tests	495 points
Other	45 points

Grade Points

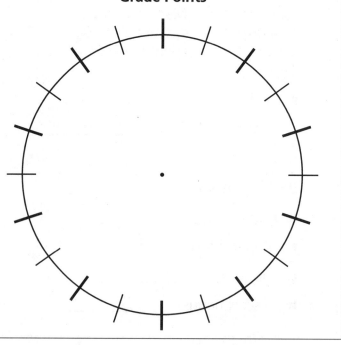

Reading Circle Graphs

Use the circle graphs to find each answer.

1. The circle graph shows how many cents out of each dollar of federal income is from each source. The total income for the year was $600,000,000,000. How much money was from each source?

**Sources of Federal Income
(out of each dollar)**

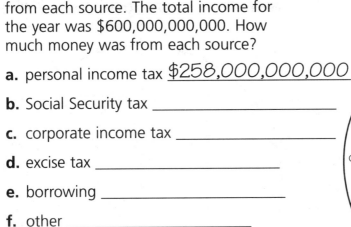

a. personal income tax $258,000,000,000

b. Social Security tax _____

c. corporate income tax _____

d. excise tax _____

e. borrowing _____

f. other _____

---

2. The circle graph shows how many cents out of each dollar that Tim spends on his car is spent on each item. He spent $5,000 on his car during the year. How much did he spend on each of the following?

**Automobile Expenses
(out of each dollar)**

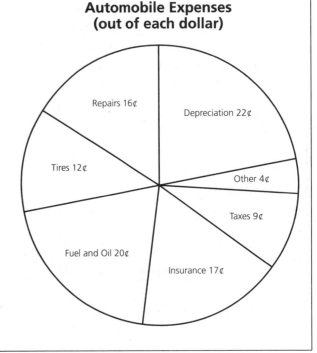

a. depreciation _____

b. repairs _____

c. tires _____

d. fuel and oil _____

e. insurance _____

f. taxes _____

g. other _____

Constructing Circle Graphs

Use the given information to construct each circle graph. The heavy marks on the circle divide the circle into 10 equal parts (10% of the circle). The lighter marks are halfway between the heavy marks. Round values to the nearest cent.

1. Construct a circle graph showing how many cents out of each dollar of federal expenditure is for each item. The total year expenditure was $650,000,000,000.

Benefit payments	$253,500,000,000
Defense	$156,000,000,000
Grants	$104,000,000,000
Net Interest	$58,500,000,000
Other	$78,000,000,000

Federal Expenditures (out of each dollar)

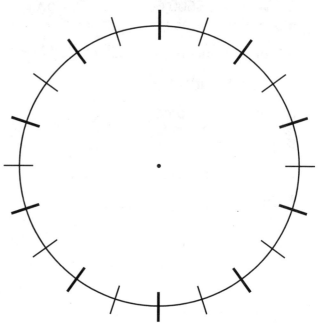

2. Use the information below to construct a circle graph showing how many cents out of each dollar of family expenditure is spent on each item. The total income is $35,000.

Food	$5,950
Shelter	$7,700
Utilities	$3,150
Clothing	$3,850
Transportation	$3,150
Personal care	$2,450
Recreation	$1,750
Savings	$1,750
Miscellaneous	$5,250

Family Expenditures (out of each dollar)

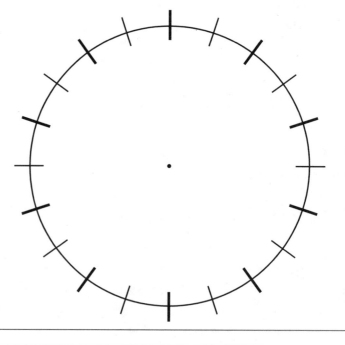

Reading Circle Graphs

Use the circle graphs to find each answer.

1. The circle graph shows the percent of sales for several products sold by a company. Total sales were $388,000,000. What amount was sold in each category?

   a. cane sugar *$93,120,000*

   b. molasses _____

   c. cigars _____

   d. candy _____

   e. other _____

Sales

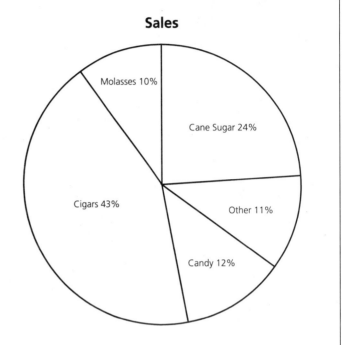

Molasses 10%

Cane Sugar 24%

Cigars 43%

Other 11%

Candy 12%

2. The circle graph shows the percent of sales for several products sold by a company. Total sales were $492,000,000. What amount was sold in each category?

   a. paper and paperboard _____

   b. towels and napkins _____

   c. cartons _____

   d. matches _____

   e. building products _____

Sales

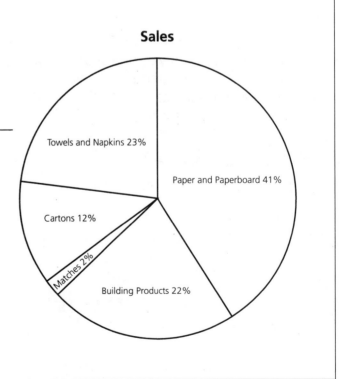

Towels and Napkins 23%

Paper and Paperboard 41%

Cartons 12%

Matches 2%

Building Products 22%

Constructing Circle Graphs

Use the given information to construct each circle graph. The heavy marks on the circle divide the circle into 10 equal parts (10% of the circle). The lighter marks are halfway between the heavy marks. Round values to the nearest percent.

1. The figures below indicate the sales for a company in one year. Construct a circle graph showing the sales for each product. The amounts shown are in millions of dollars.

Cane sugar	$142
Molasses	$30
Cigars	$170
Candy	$43
Other	$55

Sales

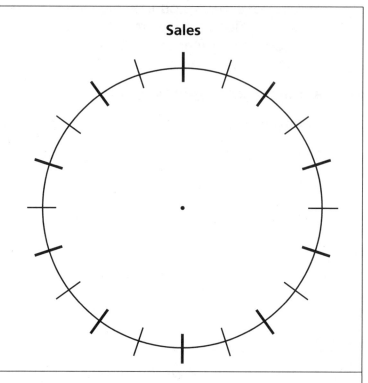

2. The figures below indicate the sales for a company in one year. Construct a circle graph showing the sales for each category. The amounts shown are in millions of dollars.

Paper and paperboard	$194
Towels and napkins	$107
Cartons	$55
Matches	$9
Building products	$89

Sales

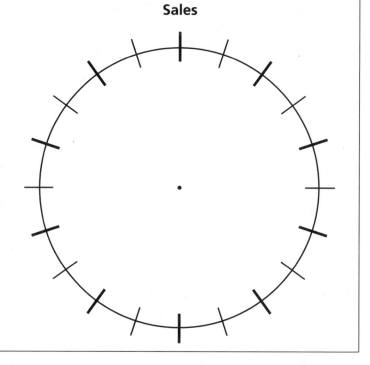

Reading Circle Graphs

Use the circle graphs to find each answer.

1. The circle graph shows where each dollar spent on cosmetics goes. Total sales one year were $20,000,000. How many dollars went to each of the following?

   a. manufacturer <u>$12,000,000</u>

   b. retailer _____

   c. packaging _____

   d. ingredients _____

   e. wages and salaries _____

   f. promotion _____

   g. profit _____

   h. interest _____

Cosmetics: Income and Expenses (out of each dollar)

MANUFACTURER 60¢
Promotion 10¢
Wages and Salaries 19¢
Ingredients 8¢
Interest 2¢
Packaging 11¢
Profit 10¢
Expenses and Profit 40¢
RETAILER 40¢

2. The circle graph shows the percent of total oil exports for the countries shown. The total value of the exports was $130,000,000,000. How many dollars worth of oil were exported from each country?

   a. Saudi Arabia _____

   b. Libya _____

   c. Nigeria _____

   d. United Arab Emirates _____

   e. Kuwait _____

   f. Indonesia _____

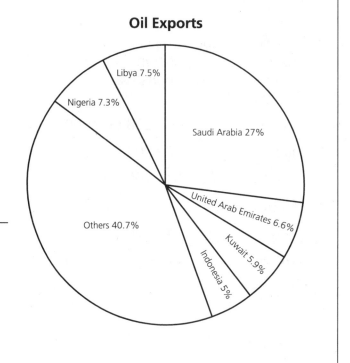

Oil Exports

Libya 7.5%
Nigeria 7.3%
Saudi Arabia 27%
United Arab Emirates 6.6%
Others 40.7%
Kuwait 5.9%
Indonesia 5%

Constructing Circle Graphs

Use the given information to construct each circle graph. The heavy marks on the circle divide the circle into 10 equal parts (10% of the circle). The lighter marks are halfway between the heavy marks. Round values to the nearest tenth of a percent.

1. Construct a circle graph showing the percentage of the total cost of choice beef going to each source. The dollar amounts are based on a price of $2.23 per pound.

Farmer	$1.47
Transportation to slaughterhouse	$0.02
Slaughterhouse	$0.06
Intercity transportation	$0.02
Wholesaler	$0.09
Retailer	$0.57

Choice Beef: Income and Expenses

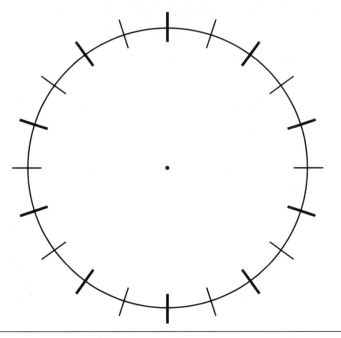

2. Construct a circle graph showing the percentage of oil imports for each country shown. The value of the oil imports was $120,000,000,000.

United States	$42,200,000,000
Japan	$23,900,000,000
West Germany	$14,100,000,000
France	$11,100,000,000
Italy	$8,000,000,000
Other	$20,700,000,000

Oil Imports

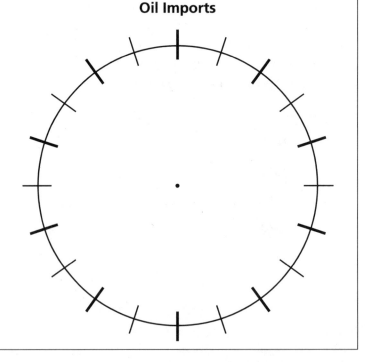

Basic Computation Series 2000: Applying Computational Skills

Reading Circle Graphs

Use the circle graphs to find each answer.

1. The circle graph shows the percent
   of workers in each job category in
   Hawaii. There are 212,000 workers.
   How many are in each category?

   a. trade _____40,280_____

   b. manufacturing _____

   c. professional services _____

   d. government _____

   e. construction _____

   f. transportation, communication,
   and utilities _____

   g. other _____

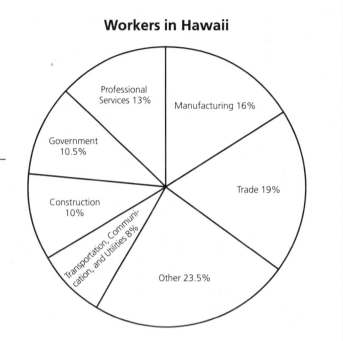

Workers in Hawaii

Professional Services 13%
Manufacturing 16%
Government 10.5%
Construction 10%
Trade 19%
Transportation, Communication, and Utilities 8%
Other 23.5%

2. The circle graph shows the percent
   of workers in each job category in
   Iowa. There are 1,000,000 workers.
   How many are in each category?

   a. agriculture _____

   b. trade _____

   c. manufacturing _____

   d. professional services _____

   e. transportation, communication,
   and utilities _____

   f. construction _____

   g. other _____

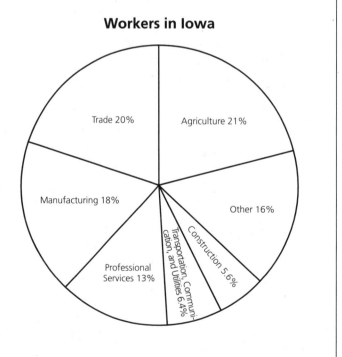

Workers in Iowa

Trade 20%
Agriculture 21%
Manufacturing 18%
Other 16%
Professional Services 13%
Transportation, Communication, and Utilities 6.4%
Construction 5.6%

Constructing Circle Graphs

Use the given information to construct each circle graph. The heavy marks on the circle divide the circle into 10 equal parts (10% of the circle). The lighter marks are halfway between the heavy marks. Round values to the nearest tenth of a percent.

1. Construct a circle graph showing the percentage of workers in the state of New York engaged in the indicated job categories. There are 6,600,000 workers in the state.

Manufacturing	1,875,000
Trade	1,000,000
Professional services	870,000
Transportation, communication, and utilities	500,000
Finance, insurance, and real estate	400,000
Personal services	375,000
Other	1,580,000

Workers in New York

2. Construct a circle graph showing the percent of workers in the state of Texas engaged in the indicated job categories. There are 3,300,000 workers in the state.

Trade	700,000
Manufacturing	550,000
Professional services	375,000
Agriculture	300,000
Personal services	260,000
Construction	250,000
Other	865,000

Workers in Texas

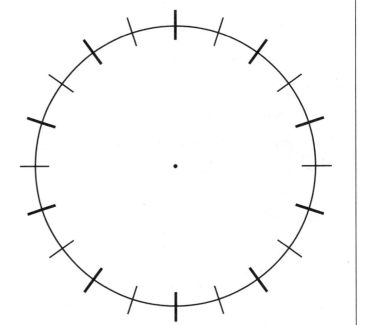

Reading Maps

Use the **MAP OF LINCOLN COUNTY** on page 126 to find each distance. Towns are indicated by letters such as **A, B, C,** or **AA, BB, CC.** Measure the shortest distance between towns along marked roads. Measure from the center of one circle or diamond to the center of the next, measuring to the nearest millimeter. Solve a proportion to find an approximation of each actual distance to the nearest tenth of a kilometer.

1. from NN to LL

map measurement: ____29____ mm

actual distance: ___72.5___ km

2. from B to P

map measurement: _____ mm

actual distance: _____ km

3. from A to ZZ

map measurement: _____ mm

actual distance: _____ km

4. from L to GG

map measurement: _____ mm

actual distance: _____ km

5. from H to J

map measurement: _____ mm

actual distance: _____ km

Reading Maps

Use the **MAP OF LINCOLN COUNTY** on page 126 to find each distance. Towns are indicated by letters such as **A, B, C,** or **AA, BB, CC.** Measure the shortest distance between towns along marked roads. Measure from the center of one circle or diamond to the center of the next, measuring to the nearest millimeter. Solve a proportion to find an approximation of each actual distance to the nearest tenth of a kilometer.

---

1. from NN to QQ

   map measurement: _____73_____ mm

   actual distance: __182.5__ km

---

2. from TT to XX

   map measurement: _____ mm

   actual distance: _____ km

---

3. from P to HH

   map measurement: _____ mm

   actual distance: _____ km

---

4. from A to II

   map measurement: _____ mm

   actual distance: _____ km

---

5. from PP to YY

   map measurement: _____ mm

   actual distance: _____ km

Reading Maps

Use the MAP OF LINCOLN COUNTY on page 126 to find each distance. Towns are indicated by letters such as A, B, C, or AA, BB, CC. Measure the shortest distance between towns along marked roads. Measure from the center of one circle or diamond to the center of the next, measuring to the nearest millimeter. Solve a proportion to find an approximation of each actual distance to the nearest tenth of a kilometer.

1. from AA to NN

   map measurement: _____32_____ mm

   actual distance: __80.0__ km

2. from O to HH

   map measurement: _____ mm

   actual distance: _____ km

3. from V to MM

   map measurement: _____ mm

   actual distance: _____ km

4. from I to QQ

   map measurement: _____ mm

   actual distance: _____ km

5. from N to GG

   map measurement: _____ mm

   actual distance: _____ km

Reading Maps

Use the **MAP OF LINCOLN COUNTY on page 126** to find each distance. **Towns are indicated by letters such as A, B, C, or AA, BB, CC. Measure the shortest distance between towns along marked roads. Measure from the center of one circle or diamond to the center of the next, measuring to the nearest millimeter. Solve a proportion to find an approximation of each actual distance to the nearest tenth of a kilometer.**

1. from LL to ZZ

map measurement: _____93_____ mm

actual distance: __232.5__ km

2. from AA to TT

map measurement: _____ mm

actual distance: _____ km

3. from E to LL

map measurement: _____ mm

actual distance: _____ km

4. from EE to RR

map measurement: _____ mm

actual distance: _____ km

5. from H to B

map measurement: _____ mm

actual distance: _____ km

Reading Maps

Use the **MAP OF LINCOLN COUNTY** on page 126 to find each distance. Towns are indicated by letters such as A, B, C, or AA, BB, CC. Measure the shortest distance between towns along marked roads. Measure from the center of one circle or diamond to the center of the next, measuring to the nearest millimeter. Solve a proportion to find an approximation of each actual distance to the nearest tenth of a kilometer.

1. from AA to U

map measurement: ___38___ mm

actual distance: ___95.0___ km

2. from A to N

map measurement: _____ mm

actual distance: _____ km

3. from L to ZZ

map measurement: _____ mm

actual distance: _____ km

4. from S to XX

map measurement: _____ mm

actual distance: _____ km

5. from DD to WW

map measurement: _____ mm

actual distance: _____ km

Reading Maps

Use the **MAP OF LINCOLN COUNTY** on page 126 to find each distance. Towns are indicated by letters such as A, B, C, or AA, BB, CC. Measure the shortest distance between towns along marked roads. Measure from the center of one circle or diamond to the center of the next, measuring to the nearest millimeter. Solve a proportion to find an approximation of each actual distance to the nearest tenth of a kilometer.

1. from B to YY

map measurement: ___134___ mm

actual distance: __335.0__ km

2. from E to O

map measurement: _____ mm

actual distance: _____ km

3. from B to LL

map measurement: _____ mm

actual distance: _____ km

4. from V to AA

map measurement: _____ mm

actual distance: _____ km

5. from RR to W

map measurement: _____ mm

actual distance: _____ km

Basic Computation Series 2000: Applying Computational Skills

SECTION 2 Graphs and Maps

Reading Maps

Use the MAP OF LINCOLN COUNTY on page 126 to find each distance. Towns are indicated by letters such as A, B, C, or AA, BB, CC. Measure the shortest distance between towns along marked roads. Measure from the center of one circle or diamond to the center of the next, measuring to the nearest millimeter. Solve a proportion to find an approximation of each actual distance to the nearest tenth of a kilometer.

1. from A to O

   map measurement: ___39___ mm

   actual distance: __97.5__ km

2. from Z to LL

   map measurement: _____ mm

   actual distance: _____ km

3. from P to ZZ

   map measurement: _____ mm

   actual distance: _____ km

4. from Z to L

   map measurement: _____ mm

   actual distance: _____ km

5. from PP to KK

   map measurement: _____ mm

   actual distance: _____ km

Reading Maps

Use the MAP OF LINCOLN COUNTY on page 126 to find each distance. Towns are indicated by letters such as A, B, C, or AA, BB, CC. Measure the shortest distance between towns along marked roads. Measure from the center of one circle or diamond to the center of the next, measuring to the nearest millimeter. Solve a proportion to find an approximation of each actual distance to the nearest tenth of a kilometer.

1. from GG to W

map measurement: ___109___ mm

actual distance: __272.5__ km

2. from I to TT

map measurement: _____ mm

actual distance: _____ km

3. from B to ZZ

map measurement: _____ mm

actual distance: _____ km

4. from A to JJ

map measurement: _____ mm

actual distance: _____ km

5. from D to XX

map measurement: _____ mm

actual distance: _____ km

Reading Maps

Use the **MAP OF LINCOLN COUNTY on page 126** to find each distance. Towns are indicated by letters such as A, B, C, or AA, BB, CC. Measure the shortest distance between towns along marked roads. Measure from the center of one circle or diamond to the center of the next, measuring to the nearest millimeter. Solve a proportion to find an approximation of each actual distance to the nearest tenth of a kilometer.

1. from OO to W

map measurement: _____57_____ mm

actual distance: __142.5__ km

2. from V to LL

map measurement: _____ mm

actual distance: _____ km

3. from D to KK

map measurement: _____ mm

actual distance: _____ km

4. from N to YY

map measurement: _____ mm

actual distance: _____ km

5. from C to W

map measurement: _____ mm

actual distance: _____ km

Reading Maps

Use the **MAP OF LINCOLN COUNTY** on page 126 to find each distance. Towns are indicated by letters such as A, B, C, or AA, BB, CC. Measure the shortest distance between towns along marked roads. Measure from the center of one circle or diamond to the center of the next, measuring to the nearest millimeter. Solve a proportion to find an approximation of each actual distance to the nearest tenth of a kilometer.

1. from I to NN

   map measurement: ____111____ mm

   actual distance: __277.5__ km

2. from B to JJ

   map measurement: _____ mm

   actual distance: _____ km

3. from TT to ZZ

   map measurement: _____ mm

   actual distance: _____ km

4. from AA to GG

   map measurement: _____ mm

   actual distance: _____ km

5. from FF to E

   map measurement: _____ mm

   actual distance: _____ km

Consumer Topics

One very important life skill is the ability to make change. The change received from a purchase is the difference between the amount tendered and the amount of the purchase. The most efficient change is that which requires the least number of coins and bills.

Example 1: The purchase price of an item is $7.95. How much change is due from a $20 bill? Complete the table to indicate the most efficient change.

Solution: The change due is $20.00 − $7.95; that is, $12.05. Coins are used to bring the change due down to $12. That requires 1 nickel. Twelve dollars is 1 ten dollar bill plus 2 one dollar bills.

Amount Received	Change Due	Most Efficient Change						
		$10	$5	$1	25¢	10¢	5¢	1¢
$20.00	$12.05	1		2			1	

Example 2: The purchase price of an item is $11.49. How much change is due from $15.50? Complete the table to indicate the most efficient change.

Solution: The change due is $15.50 − $11.49; that is, $4.01. One penny brings the change due down to $4. The remaining change is 4 one dollar bills.

Amount Received	Change Due	Most Efficient Change						
		$10	$5	$1	25¢	10¢	5¢	1¢
$15.50	$4.01			4				1

The *unit price* of an item is the price of a single unit of a particular measure of the item. Unit prices are often used to determine the "best buy" for a certain item to be purchased. Unit prices are determined by dividing the given price of the item by the number of units of standard measure it contains. The less the unit price of an item, the better buy it is.

Example 3: Listed below are the prices for three different-sized bottles of cooking oil. Find the unit price for each item to the nearest tenth of a cent. Then decide which is the best buy.

    a. 20 oz, $0.89   **b.** 32 oz, $1.09   **c.** 48 oz, $2.29

Solution: Find the unit prices by dividing the price of each bottle by the number of ounces it contains. Round each unit price to the nearest tenth of a cent. (Note: The symbol "≈" means "approximately equal to.")

    a. $0.89 \div 20 \approx 0.045$. Thus, the unit price is 4.5¢ per ounce.

    b. $1.09 \div 32 \approx 0.034$. Thus, the unit price is 3.4¢ per ounce.

    c. $2.29 \div 48 \approx 0.048$. Thus, the unit price is 4.8¢ per ounce.

Comparing unit prices, the best buy is **b**, 32 oz for $1.09.

Example 4: Listed below are the prices for three different-sized bags of frozen peas. Find the unit price for each item to the nearest tenth of a cent. Then decide which is the best buy.

    a. 10 oz, $0.43   **b.** 16 oz, $0.68   **c.** 20 oz, $0.79

Solution: Find the unit prices by dividing the price of each package by the number of ounces it contains.

    a. $0.43 \div 10 \approx 0.043$. Thus, the unit price is 4.3¢ per ounce.

    b. $0.68 \div 16 \approx 0.043$. Thus, the unit price is 4.3¢ per ounce.

    c. $0.79 \div 20 \approx 0.040$. Thus, the unit price is 4.0¢ per ounce.

Comparing unit prices, the best buy is **c**, 20 oz for $0.79.

Making Change

Complete the table for each purchase price.

Purchase price: $4.31

Amount Received	Change Due	Most Efficient Change						
		$10	$5	$1	25¢	10¢	5¢	1¢
1. $20.00	$15.69	1	1		2	1	1	4
2. $10.00								
3. $5.00								
4. $5.35								
5. $4.50								

Purchase price: $7.57

Amount Received	Change Due	Most Efficient Change						
		$10	$5	$1	25¢	10¢	5¢	1¢
6. $20.00								
7. $10.00								
8. $12.57								
9. $10.60								
10. $8.00								

Comparing Unit Prices

Find the unit price for each item to the nearest tenth of a cent. Then circle the unit price that is the best buy.

1. Facial tissue

    a. box of 50, $0.25 __0.5¢ each__

    b. box of 100, $0.35 __0.4¢ each__

    c. box of 200, $0.59 (0.3¢ each)

2. Toothpaste

    a. 3 oz, $0.49 _____

    b. 5 oz, $0.99 _____

    c. 6.4 oz, $1.09 _____

3. Bath soap

    a. 3 oz, $0.20 _____

    b. 5 oz, $0.25 _____

    c. 7 oz, $0.40 _____

4. Liquid detergent

    a. 16 oz, $0.69 _____

    b. 32 oz, $1.49 _____

    c. 64 oz, $2.69 _____

5. Shortening

    a. 16 oz, $0.69 _____

    b. 32 oz, $1.44 _____

    c. 48 oz, $2.19 _____

6. Hair spray

    a. 7 oz, $0.89 _____

    b. 9 oz, $1.09 _____

    c. 11 oz, $1.39 _____

7. Shampoo

    a. 12 oz, $1.49 _____

    b. 15 oz, $1.69 _____

    c. 20 oz, $2.29 _____

8. Dill pickles

    a. 12 oz, $0.49 _____

    b. 22 oz, $0.79 _____

    c. 32 oz, $1.09 _____

9. Pineapple

    a. 16 oz, $0.49 _____

    b. 20 oz, $0.57 _____

    c. 26 oz, $0.79 _____

10. Plastic wrap

    a. 50 ft, $0.39 _____

    b. 100 ft, $0.60 _____

    c. 200 ft, $1.09 _____

Making Change

Complete the table for each purchase price.

Purchase price: $14.17

Amount Received	Change Due	Most Efficient Change						
		$10	$5	$1	25¢	10¢	5¢	1¢
1. $20.00	$5.83		1		3		1	3
2. $15.25								
3. $15.17								
4. $15.00								
5. $59.42								

Purchase price: $42.53

Amount Received	Change Due	Most Efficient Change						
		$10	$5	$1	25¢	10¢	5¢	1¢
6. $50.00								
7. $50.53								
8. $45.00								
9. $45.05								
10. $43.00								

Comparing Unit Prices

Find the unit price for each item to the nearest tenth of a cent. Then circle the unit price that is the best buy.

1. Vegetable juice

   a. 4 oz, $0.15 _3.8¢ per oz_

   b. 12 oz, $0.39 _3.3¢ per oz_

   c. 32 oz, $0.77 (2.4¢ per oz)

2. Trash bags

   a. box of 15, $1.79 _____

   b. box of 20, $1.99 _____

   c. box of 40, $2.99 _____

3. Face lotion

   a. 6 oz, $3.99 _____

   b. 8 oz, $5.59 _____

   c. 12 oz, $7.99 _____

4. Envelopes

   a. box of 50, $0.89 _____

   b. box of 100, $1.49 _____

   c. box of 200, $2.79 _____

5. Deodorant

   a. 4 oz, $1.29 _____

   b. 6 oz, $1.99 _____

   c. 12 oz, $2.79 _____

6. Paper plates

   a. box of 50, $0.50 _____

   b. box of 100, $1.29 _____

   c. box of 200, $2.49 _____

7. Nasal spray

   a. 12 mL, $1.49 _____

   b. 15 mL, $1.69 _____

   c. 18 mL, $2.29 _____

8. Vitamin tablets

   a. bottle of 100, $5.69 _____

   b. bottle of 200, $7.95 _____

   c. bottle of 500, $23.00 _____

9. Window cleaner

   a. 10 oz, $0.59 _____

   b. 15 oz, $0.79 _____

   c. 24 oz, $1.32 _____

10. Gift wrap

   a. 40 ft^2, $0.99 _____

   b. 80 ft^2, $2.49 _____

   c. 150 ft^2, $4.29 _____

Making Change

Complete the table for each purchase price.

Purchase price: $4.38

Amount Received	Change Due	Most Efficient Change						
		$10	$5	$1	25¢	10¢	5¢	1¢
1. $50.00	$45.62	4	1		2	1		2
2. $20.00								
3. $25.75								
4. $5.00								
5. $10.50								

Purchase price: $6.89

Amount Received	Change Due	Most Efficient Change						
		$10	$5	$1	25¢	10¢	5¢	1¢
6. $39.50								
7. $26.75								
8. $20.00								
9. $10.90								
10. $7.00								

Comparing Unit Prices

Find the unit price for each item to the nearest tenth of a cent. Then circle the unit price that is the best buy.

1. Facial tissue

    a. box of 50, $0.29 _0.6¢ each_

    b. box of 100, $0.36 _0.4¢ each_

    c. box of 200, $0.49 _0.2¢ each_

2. Toothpaste

    a. 3 oz, $0.68 _____

    b. 5 oz, $1.05 _____

    c. 6.4 oz, $1.19 _____

3. Bath soap

    a. 3 oz, $0.18 _____

    b. 5 oz, $0.32 _____

    c. 7 oz, $0.59 _____

4. Liquid detergent

    a. 16 oz, $0.89 _____

    b. 32 oz, $1.29 _____

    c. 64 oz, $2.39 _____

5. Shortening

    a. 16 oz, $0.67 _____

    b. 32 oz, $1.49 _____

    c. 48 oz, $2.29 _____

6. Hair spray

    a. 7 oz, $0.99 _____

    b. 9 oz, $1.19 _____

    c. 11 oz, $1.69 _____

7. Shampoo

    a. 12 oz, $1.39 _____

    b. 15 oz, $1.55 _____

    c. 20 oz, $2.39 _____

8. Dill pickles

    a. 12 oz, $0.45 _____

    b. 22 oz, $0.75 _____

    c. 32 oz, $1.00 _____

9. Pineapple

    a. 16 oz, $0.39 _____

    b. 20 oz, $0.65 _____

    c. 26 oz, $1.29 _____

10. Plastic wrap

    a. 50 ft, $0.19 _____

    b. 100 ft, $0.49 _____

    c. 200 ft, $1.19 _____

Making Change

Complete the table for each purchase price.

Purchase price: $11.71

Amount Received	Change Due	Most Efficient Change						
		$10	$5	$1	25¢	10¢	5¢	1¢
1. $45.00	$33.29	3		3	1			4
2. $27.50								
3. $15.75								
4. $12.00								
5. $15.00								

Purchase price: $36.22

Amount Received	Change Due	Most Efficient Change						
		$10	$5	$1	25¢	10¢	5¢	1¢
6. $151.80								
7. $75.00								
8. $60.00								
9. $40.25								
10. $37.50								

Comparing Unit Prices

Find the unit price for each item to the nearest tenth of a cent. Then circle the unit price that is the best buy.

1. Vegetable juice

    a. 4 oz, $0.32 _8.0¢ per oz_

    b. 12 oz, $0.64 _5.3¢ per oz_

    c. 32 oz, $0.99 (3.1¢ per oz)

2. Trash bags

    a. box of 15, $1.35 _____

    b. box of 20, $1.99 _____

    c. box of 40, $2.99 _____

3. Face lotion

    a. 6 oz, $4.89 _____

    b. 8 oz, $6.39 _____

    c. 12 oz, $10.50 _____

4. Envelopes

    a. box of 50, $1.39

    b. box of 100, $2.10 _____

    c. box of 200, $2.89 _____

5. Deodorant

    a. 4 oz, $1.49 _____

    b. 6 oz, $1.79 _____

    c. 12 oz, $2.89 _____

6. Paper plates

    a. box of 50, $0.65 _____

    b. box of 100, $1.19 _____

    c. box of 200, $2.89 _____

7. Nasal spray

    a. 12 mL, $1.75 _____

    b. 15 mL, $1.89 _____

    c. 18 mL, $2.69 _____

8. Vitamin tablets

    a. bottle of 100, $5.99 _____

    b. bottle of 200, $7.99 _____

    c. bottle of 500, $22.49 _____

9. Window cleaner

    a. 10 oz, $0.69 _____

    b. 15 oz, $0.89 _____

    c. 24 oz, $1.45 _____

10. Gift wrap

    a. 40 ft^2, $1.29 _____

    b. 80 ft^2, $2.79 _____

    c. 150 ft^2, $4.39 _____

Basic Computation Series 2000: Applying Computational Skills

SECTION 3 Consumer Topics

Making Change

Complete the table for each purchase price.

Purchase price: $3.75

Amount Received	Change Due	Most Efficient Change						
		$10	$5	$1	25¢	10¢	5¢	1¢
1. $20.00	$16.25	1	1	1	1			
2. $10.00								
3. $5.00								
4. $5.75								
5. $4.00								

Purchase price: $8.23

Amount Received	Change Due	Most Efficient Change						
		$10	$5	$1	25¢	10¢	5¢	1¢
6. $50.00								
7. $20.00								
8. $10.00								
9. $10.23								
10. $9.00								

Comparing Unit Prices

Find the unit price for each item to the nearest tenth of a cent. Then circle the unit price that is the best buy.

1. Facial tissue

    a. box of 50, $0.35 _0.7¢ each_

    b. box of 100, $0.54 _0.5¢ each_

    c. box of 200, $0.64 (0.3¢ each)

2. Toothpaste

    a. 3 oz, $0.79 _____

    b. 5 oz, $1.25 _____

    c. 6.4 oz, $1.32 _____

3. Bath soap

    a. 3 oz, $0.25 _____

    b. 5 oz, $0.39 _____

    c. 7 oz, $0.62 _____

4. Liquid detergent

    a. 16 oz, $0.93 _____

    b. 32 oz, $1.35 _____

    c. 64 oz, $2.79 _____

5. Shortening

    a. 16 oz, $0.48 _____

    b. 32 oz, $1.62 _____

    c. 48 oz, $2.59 _____

6. Hair spray

    a. 7 oz, $1.22 _____

    b. 9 oz, $1.35 _____

    c. 11 oz, $1.89 _____

7. Shampoo

    a. 12 oz, $1.55 _____

    b. 15 oz, $1.89 _____

    c. 20 oz, $2.89 _____

8. Dill pickles

    a. 12 oz, $0.61 _____

    b. 22 oz, $0.82 _____

    c. 32 oz, $1.10 _____

9. Pineapple

    a. 16 oz, $0.51 _____

    b. 20 oz, $0.83 _____

    c. 26 oz, $1.61 _____

10. Plastic wrap

    a. 50 ft, $0.22 _____

    b. 100 ft, $0.51 _____

    c. 200 ft, $1.23 _____

Making Change

Complete the table for each purchase price.

Purchase price: $15.42

Amount Received	Change Due	Most Efficient Change						
		$10	$5	$1	25¢	10¢	5¢	1¢
1. $50.00	$34.58	3		4	2		1	3
2. $20.00								
3. $20.42								
4. $16.00								
5. $32.59								

Purchase price: $36.80

Amount Received	Change Due	Most Efficient Change						
		$10	$5	$1	25¢	10¢	5¢	1¢
6. $50.00								
7. $40.00								
8. $42.00								
9. $41.80								
10. $51.80								

Comparing Unit Prices

Find the unit price for each item to the nearest tenth of a cent. Then circle the unit price that is the best buy.

1. Vegetable juice

  a. 4 oz, $0.39 _9.8¢ per oz_

  b. 12 oz, $0.64 _5.3¢ per oz_

  c. 32 oz, $0.79 _2.5¢ per oz_ (circled)

2. Trash bags

  a. box of 15, $1.45 _____

  b. box of 20, $1.89 _____

  c. box of 40, $2.85 _____

3. Face lotion

  a. 6 oz, $4.79 _____

  b. 8 oz, $6.85 _____

  c. 12 oz, $9.95 _____

4. Envelopes

  a. box of 50, $1.61 _____

  b. box of 100, $2.35 _____

  c. box of 200, $2.92 _____

5. Deodorant

  a. 4 oz, $1.75 _____

  b. 6 oz, $1.93 _____

  c. 12 oz, $2.99 _____

6. Paper plates

  a. box of 50, $0.59 _____

  b. box of 100, $1.35 _____

  c. box of 200, $2.61 _____

7. Nasal spray

  a. 12 mL, $1.83 _____

  b. 15 mL, $1.99 _____

  c. 18 mL, $2.59 _____

8. Vitamin tablets

  a. bottle of 100, $6.13 _____

  b. bottle of 200, $8.25 _____

  c. bottle of 500, $24.59 _____

9. Window cleaner

  a. 10 oz, $0.81 _____

  b. 15 oz, $0.95 _____

  c. 24 oz, $1.62 _____

10. Gift wrap

  a. 40 ft^2, $1.49 _____

  b. 80 ft^2, $2.85 _____

  c. 150 ft^2, $5.00 _____

Making Change

Complete the table for each purchase price.

Purchase price: $2.68

Amount Received	Change Due	Most Efficient Change						
		$10	$5	$1	25¢	10¢	5¢	1¢
1. $20.00	$17.32	1	1	2	1		1	2
2. $10.00								
3. $5.00								
4. $5.68								
5. $3.00								

Purchase price: $8.32

Amount Received	Change Due	Most Efficient Change						
		$10	$5	$1	25¢	10¢	5¢	1¢
6. $20.00								
7. $13.32								
8. $10.32								
9. $10.00								
10. $8.50								

Comparing Unit Prices

Find the unit price for each item to the nearest tenth of a cent. Then circle the unit price that is the best buy.

1. Facial tissue

   a. box of 50, $0.19 _0.4¢ each_

   b. box of 100, $0.34 (0.3¢ each)

   c. box of 200, $0.91 _0.5¢ each_

6. Hair spray

   a. 7 oz, $0.99 _____

   b. 9 oz, $1.29 _____

   c. 11 oz, $1.89 _____

2. Toothpaste

   a. 3 oz, $0.69 _____

   b. 5 oz, $1.09 _____

   c. 6.4 oz, $1.45 _____

7. Shampoo

   a. 12 oz, $1.98 _____

   b. 15 oz, $2.29 _____

   c. 20 oz, $2.89 _____

3. Bath soap

   a. 3 oz, $0.35 _____

   b. 5 oz, $0.39 _____

   c. 7 oz, $0.50 _____

8. Dill pickles

   a. 12 oz, $0.29 _____

   b. 22 oz, $0.69 _____

   c. 32 oz, $1.19 _____

4. Liquid detergent

   a. 16 oz, $0.49 _____

   b. 32 oz, $1.29 _____

   c. 64 oz, $2.50 _____

9. Pineapple

   a. 16 oz, $0.89 _____

   b. 20 oz, $0.99 _____

   c. 26 oz, $1.39 _____

5. Shortening

   a. 16 oz, $0.39 _____

   b. 32 oz, $0.98 _____

   c. 48 oz, $2.09 _____

10. Plastic wrap

   a. 50 ft, $0.53 _____

   b. 100 ft, $0.90 _____

   c. 200 ft, $1.19 _____

Making Change

Complete the table for each purchase price.

Purchase price: $27.57

Amount Received	Change Due	Most Efficient Change						
		$10	$5	$1	25¢	10¢	5¢	1¢
1. $40.00	$12.43	1		2	1	1	1	3
2. $32.57								
3. $30.57								
4. $30.00								
5. $28.00								

Purchase price: $36.92

Amount Received	Change Due	Most Efficient Change						
		$10	$5	$1	25¢	10¢	5¢	1¢
6. $50.00								
7. $40.00								
8. $41.92								
9. $40.92								
10. $37.00								

Comparing Unit Prices

Find the unit price for each item to the nearest tenth of a cent. Then circle the unit price that is the best buy.

1. Vegetable juice

  a. 4 oz, $0.29 _7.3¢ per oz_

  b. 12 oz, $0.59 _4.9¢ per oz_

  c. 32 oz, $0.75 (2.3¢ per oz)

2. Trash bags

  a. box of 15, $1.29 _____

  b. box of 20, $1.79 _____

  c. box of 40, $2.89 _____

3. Face lotion

  a. 6 oz, $5.00 _____

  b. 8 oz, $6.50 _____

  c. 12 oz, $8.49 _____

4. Envelopes

  a. box of 50, $0.29 _____

  b. box of 100, $1.00 _____

  c. box of 200, $2.49 _____

5. Deodorant

  a. 4 oz, $0.69 _____

  b. 6 oz, $1.59 _____

  c. 12 oz, $2.29 _____

6. Paper plates

  a. box of 50, $0.89 _____

  b. box of 100, $1.45 _____

  c. box of 200, $3.12 _____

7. Nasal spray

  a. 12 mL, $1.09 _____

  b. 15 mL, $1.49 _____

  c. 18 mL, $2.39 _____

8. Vitamin tablets

  a. bottle of 100, $3.29 _____

  b. bottle of 200, $6.29 _____

  c. bottle of 500, $18.00 _____

9. Window cleaner

  a. 10 oz, $0.89 _____

  b. 15 oz, $0.98 _____

  c. 24 oz, $1.09 _____

10. Gift wrap

  a. 40 ft^2, $0.49 _____

  b. 80 ft^2, $1.99 _____

  c. 150 ft^2, $3.99 _____

Making Change

Complete the table for each purchase price.

Purchase price: $2.71

Amount Received	Change Due	Most Efficient Change						
		$10	$5	$1	25¢	10¢	5¢	1¢
1. $20.00	$17.29	1	1	2	1			4
2. $10.00								
3. $5.00								
4. $3.00								
5. $2.75								

Purchase price: $8.35

Amount Received	Change Due	Most Efficient Change						
		$10	$5	$1	25¢	10¢	5¢	1¢
6. $20.00								
7. $10.00								
8. $9.00								
9. $8.50								
10. $8.40								

Comparing Unit Prices

Find the unit price for each item to the nearest tenth of a cent. Then circle the unit price that is the best buy.

1. Facial tissue

   a. box of 50, $0.35 <u>0.7¢ each</u>

   b. box of 100, $0.43 <u>0.4¢ each</u>

   c. box of 200, $0.56 (0.3¢ each)

2. Toothpaste

   a. 3 oz, $0.79 _____

   b. 5 oz, $1.10 _____

   c. 6.4 oz, $1.49 _____

3. Bath soap

   a. 3 oz, $0.22 _____

   b. 5 oz, $0.43 _____

   c. 7 oz, $0.68 _____

4. Liquid detergent

   a. 16 oz, $0.84 _____

   b. 32 oz, $1.36 _____

   c. 64 oz, $2.12 _____

5. Shortening

   a. 16 oz, $0.51 _____

   b. 32 oz, $1.32 _____

   c. 48 oz, $2.25 _____

6. Hair spray

   a. 7 oz, $0.96 _____

   b. 9 oz, $1.29 _____

   c. 11 oz, $1.75 _____

7. Shampoo

   a. 12 oz, $1.43 _____

   b. 15 oz, $1.82 _____

   c. 20 oz, $2.29 _____

8. Dill pickles

   a. 12 oz, $0.51 _____

   b. 22 oz, $0.69 _____

   c. 32 oz, $1.10 _____

9. Pineapple

   a. 16 oz, $0.43 _____

   b. 20 oz, $0.61 _____

   c. 26 oz, $1.35 _____

10. Plastic wrap

   a. 50 ft, $0.21 _____

   b. 100 ft, $0.65 _____

   c. 200 ft, $1.23 _____

NAME

DATE

Making Change

Complete the table for each purchase price.

Purchase price: $17.55

Amount Received	Change Due	Most Efficient Change						
		$10	$5	$1	25¢	10¢	5¢	1¢
1. $50.00	$32.45	3		2	1	2		
2. $20.00								
3. $18.00								
4. $17.75								
5. $17.70								

Purchase price: $39.92

Amount Received	Change Due	Most Efficient Change						
		$10	$5	$1	25¢	10¢	5¢	1¢
6. $100.00								
7. $50.00								
8. $75.00								
9. $86.25								
10. $62.50								

Copyright © Dale Seymour Publications®

Basic Computation Series 2000: Applying Computational Skills
SECTION 3 Consumer Topics

89

Comparing Unit Prices

Find the unit price for each item to the nearest tenth of a cent. Then circle the unit price that is the best buy.

1. Vegetable juice

    a. 4 oz, $0.24 _6.0¢ per oz_

    b. 12 oz, $0.79 _6.6¢ per oz_

    c. 32 oz, $1.26 _3.9¢ per oz_

2. Trash bags

    a. box of 15, $1.50 _____

    b. box of 20, $2.20 _____

    c. box of 40, $3.89 _____

3. Face lotion

    a. 6 oz, $4.85 _____

    b. 8 oz, $5.69 _____

    c. 12 oz, $8.99 _____

4. Envelopes

    a. box of 50, $1.42 _____

    b. box of 100, $2.19 _____

    c. box of 200, $3.09 _____

5. Deodorant

    a. 4 oz, $1.54 _____

    b. 6 oz, $1.89 _____

    c. 12 oz, $3.89 _____

6. Paper plates

    a. box of 50, $0.85 _____

    b. box of 100, $1.35 _____

    c. box of 200, $2.99 _____

7. Nasal spray

    a. 12 mL, $1.49 _____

    b. 15 mL, $1.99 _____

    c. 18 mL, $2.59 _____

8. Vitamin tablets

    a. bottle of 100, $5.25 _____

    b. bottle of 200, $6.95 _____

    c. bottle of 500, $19.89 _____

9. Window cleaner

    a. 10 oz, $0.73 _____

    b. 15 oz, $0.95 _____

    c. 24 oz, $1.69 _____

10. Gift wrap

    a. 40 ft^2, $1.35 _____

    b. 80 ft^2, $2.49 _____

    c. 150 ft^2, $4.45 _____

Practical Problems

This section of the book contains a variety of different types of word problems. The solutions require skills taught in various sections of the *Basic Computation Series 2000.*

Among the types of problems included in this section are those concerning *interest*. Whenever money is invested or borrowed, interest is usually involved. Interest is the cost of borrowing money. It is also the value gained when money is invested. The amount of money borrowed or invested is called the *principal*. Interest is usually stated in terms of a *rate*, which is typically expressed as a certain percent per year. The formula for finding simple interest is $I = prt$, where I represents interest, p represents principal, r represents rate (expressed as a decimal), and t represents time (expressed in years).

Example 1:   Mr. Perez invested $15,000 for one year at 7.2% simple interest. What interest did he earn during the year?

Solution: First, rewrite 7.2% as the decimal 0.072. Then use the formula $I = prt$, substituting 15,000 for p, 0.072 for r, and 1 for t.

$$I = prt$$
$$I = (15,000)(0.072)(1)$$
$$I = 1,080$$

Thus, the interest earned was $1,080.

Example 2:   Elizabeth paid $2,697.50 simple interest on $16,250 that she borrowed for two years. What rate of interest did she pay?

Solution: Use the formula $I = prt$, substituting 2,697.50 for I, 16,250 for p, and 2 for t.

$$I = prt$$
$$2,697.50 = (16,250)(r)(2)$$
$$2,697.50 = 32,500r$$

Divide 2,697.50 by 32,500 to find r.

$$r = 2,697.50 \div 32,500$$
$$r = 0.083$$

Thus, the rate of interest was 8.3%.

When attempting to solve a problem, it is important to know whether the information given is enough, not enough, or more than necessary to solve the problem.

Example 3: Tell whether the information given is enough, not enough, or more than necessary to solve the following problem:

Ms. Corelli earned $540 on an investment of $3,000. What was the rate of interest paid?

Solution: The solution for this problem would involve using the formula $I = prt$. The interest (I) and the principal (p) are given in the problem. To find the rate of interest (r), the time (t) would also need to be given. Therefore, there is not enough information to solve the problem.

In considering different approaches that can be used to solve a problem, examine how the pieces of given information are related to each other and to the value in question.

Example 4: Ms. Bogdan earns $22,000 per year. She spends $6,000 of it on housing. To the nearest tenth of a percent, what percent of her earnings does she spend on housing?

Solution: This problem involves finding a rate given a base amount and a percentage of that amount. Use the formula *rate = percentage ÷ base*.

> rate = percentage ÷ base
> rate = 6,000 ÷ 22,000
> rate ≈ 0.273

Thus, Ms. Bogdan spends 27.3% of her earnings on housing.

Example 5: The enrollment at Custer County High School is 125 seniors, 162 juniors, 180 sophomores, and 226 freshmen. If there are 350 girls, how many of the students are boys?

Solution: The total enrollment at the school is 693 (125 + 162 + 180 + 226). Since 350 of the students are girls, subtract 350 from 693 to find that there are 343 boys.

Estimation involves finding an approximate, rather than an exact, answer for a problem by rounding the given numbers and using simple mental or written arithmetic to determine a reasonably accurate answer. Estimation is a useful skill to cultivate because in some cases, an approximate answer is sufficient. In other cases, estimation is useful because it provides a check on the reasonableness of an answer found by some other means.

Example 6: Which is the best estimate for the answer to the following problem?

Mr. Green sold 21 cars for a total of $163,000. What was the average price of each car?

a. $80,000   **b.** $6,000   **c.** $60,000   **d.** $8,000

Solution: The average price of each car is the total value divided by the number of cars. To find an approximate answer, it is convenient to divide 160,000 by 20. Since 160,000 ÷ 20 = 8,000, $8,000 (answer **d**) is the best estimate.

Word Problems

Solve each problem.

---

1. Tim's quiz grades for one week were 75, 92, 68, and 83. What was his average grade?

---

2. Mr. Emery has four math classes containing 28, 25, 31, and 28 students. What is the total number of students in his four classes?

---

3. Lupe invested $23,680 for 4 years at 10.5% simple interest. What were her earnings?

---

4. Ms. Goldstein plans to average 45 miles per hour on the first day of a cross-country drive. How many miles can she travel at this rate in 8 hours?

---

5. If 8 apples cost $3.92, what is the cost of each apple?

Evaluating Information

For each problem, decide whether the information given is enough, not enough, or more than necessary to solve the problem. Circle the correct answer.

1. Terri drove her motorcycle 580 miles at 50 miles per hour. It took 14.5 gallons of gasoline to make the trip. How many miles per gallon did she average?

   a. enough   **b.** not enough   **c.** more than necessary

2. Wen-Chu invested $5,000 in a Savings and Loan Association. He earned 10.5% per year on his investment. What was the total amount of interest he earned?

   a. enough   **b.** not enough   **c.** more than necessary

3. The seating capacity of Pacific Bell Park is 42,000. The home run distance to left field is 335 feet. The stadium seating is full. If 39,500 people paid to attend the game, how many people in attendance did *not* pay to see the game?

   a. enough   **b.** not enough   **c.** more than necessary

4. Roy bought $5\frac{3}{4}$ yards of velour, $1\frac{1}{2}$ yards of silk, $8\frac{1}{3}$ yards of cotton, and $2\frac{1}{12}$ yards of polyester at the local sewing center. What was the total number of yards of fabric he bought?

   a. enough   **b.** not enough   **c.** more than necessary

5. For the 1981 season, Tasha had 28 hits in 45 times at bat. She struck out 9 times. What percent of the time she was at bat did she get a hit?

   a. enough   **b.** not enough   **c.** more than necessary

Basic Computation Series 2000: Applying Computational Skills
SECTION 4 Practical Problems

Word Problems

Solve each problem.

---

1. June purchased $5\frac{1}{4}$ yards of wool, $7\frac{1}{3}$ yards of polyester, and $6\frac{1}{2}$ yards of silk. What is the total amount of fabric she bought?

---

2. Lashai had a piece of plywood that was 8 feet long. She cut off $3\frac{1}{2}$ feet of it. How long was the piece that was left?

---

3. Mr. Takahashi earns $9.25 an hour. What is his gross pay for 40 hours of work?

---

4. Morgan has a ribbon 72 inches long. How many pieces $4\frac{1}{2}$ inches long can be cut from it?

---

5. Dario has invested $2,000 at 9% interest. How much interest will he earn in one year?

Evaluating Information

For each problem, decide whether the information given is enough, not enough, or more than necessary to solve the problem. Circle the correct answer.

1. On a business trip, Arlene had expenses for transportation, lodging, food, and some miscellaneous items. Transportation cost $300, lodging cost $150, and food cost $85. What was the total amount that she spent?

   a. enough   **b.** not enough   **c.** more than necessary

2. The quarterback of the football team passed the ball 27 times during a game. He completed 16 of those passes. What was his passing average for that game?

   a. enough   **b.** not enough   **c.** more than necessary

3. Virginia wants to carpet her living room. The room is 6 by 9. How many square yards of carpet should she buy?

   a. enough   **b.** not enough   **c.** more than necessary

4. Geraldine has invested $14,000 at 18% annual interest. She keeps the entire amount invested for five years. How much interest will she earn the first year?

   a. enough   **b.** not enough   **c.** more than necessary

5. Mr. Entz used 100 gallons of gasoline to drive his truck 550 miles. How many miles per gallon did he average?

   a. enough   **b.** not enough   **c.** more than necessary

Word Problems

Solve each problem.

---

1. Lynne's weekly checks during 4 weeks were $75, $125, $80, and $115. How much did she earn during this time?

---

2. Ms. Sizemore paid $342.90 in interest on a sum of money she borrowed at an annual interest rate of 9% for 6 months. How much money did she borrow?

---

3. Larry had $7\frac{1}{2}$ cups of flour. He used $2\frac{5}{8}$ cups to bake a cake. How much flour did he have left?

---

4. J.T. has saved 75% of the money he needs to buy a stereo. If he has saved $123, how much does the stereo cost?

---

5. A kitchen floor, in the shape of a rectangle, measures 8 feet by 10 feet. How many square tiles, one foot on a side, will it take to cover the floor?

Evaluating Information

For each problem, decide whether the information given is enough, not enough, or more than necessary to solve the problem. Circle the correct answer.

1. Joni earned $450 on an investment of $6,100. What was the rate of interest paid on the investment?

   a. enough   **b.** not enough   **c.** more than necessary

2. Mrs. French drove her car 1,350 miles and averaged 28 miles per gallon. How many gallons of gasoline did she use?

   a. enough   **b.** not enough   **c.** more than necessary

3. Geneva had $12\frac{3}{8}$ yards of fabric and used $5\frac{1}{2}$ yards to make a shirt. How much of the fabric was left?

   a. enough   **b.** not enough   **c.** more than necessary

4. The San Francisco Express passenger train attains a maximum speed of 90 miles per hour as it travels west from Chicago. How long does the trip take?

   a. enough   **b.** not enough   **c.** more than necessary

5. Greeley High enrollment is made up of 315 freshmen, 275 sophomores, 236 juniors, and 210 seniors. What is the total enrollment of the school?

   a. enough   **b.** not enough   **c.** more than necessary

Word Problems

Solve each problem.

---

1. For three games of bowling, Bruce had scores of 151, 165, and 176. What was his average?

---

2. Mrs. Devine made purchases of $6.31, $7.15, $8.75, and $16.91. What was the total amount that she spent?

---

3. Mr. Kim drove 275 miles in $12\frac{1}{2}$ hours. How many miles per hour did he average for the trip?

---

4. When Dontrell borrowed $9,850 at 5.7% simple interest, his cost was $1,684.35. For what length of time was the money borrowed?

---

5. A certain cake recipe requires $3\frac{1}{2}$ cups of sugar. Adam is making $1\frac{1}{2}$ times the recipe. How much sugar will he need to use?

Evaluating Information

For each problem, decide whether the information given is enough, not enough, or more than necessary to solve the problem. Circle the correct answer.

1. In 1910 in the United States, there were 181,000 passenger cars valued at $215,340,000 and 6,000 motor trucks and buses valued at $9,660,000 for a total of 187,000 vehicles. What was the average value of each passenger car?

    a. enough   **b.** not enough   **c.** more than necessary

2. Ginny needs $3\frac{1}{2}$ yards of fabric for a shirt, $2\frac{3}{4}$ yards for a blouse, and 5 yards for a dress. How many yards of fabric should she purchase for 5 shirts?

    a. enough   **b.** not enough   **c.** more than necessary

3. What is the annual interest earned on $7,520 invested at 10% per year?

    a. enough   **b.** not enough   **c.** more than necessary

4. There were 5 A's, 7 B's, 8 C's, 4 D's, and 1 F on the mathematics final examination. What was the average grade if the scores were 90, 78, 81, 61, 70, 75, 80, 62, 83, 72, 92, 78, 40, 82, 87, 65, 95, 73, 74, 68, 88, 71, 98, 94, and 82?

    a. enough   **b.** not enough   **c.** more than necessary

5. John and Booker drove 215 miles in their automobile in 4 hours and 20 minutes. What was their average fuel consumption?

    a. enough   **b.** not enough   **c.** more than necessary

AME _____ DATE _____

Word Problems

Solve each problem.

1. In 1900 there were 2,192 passenger cars sold in the United States for a total value of $4,899,443. What was the average value of each car to the nearest dollar?

2. One month, Joanna was not able to pay her credit card balance of $1,580. The interest rate charged on that balance was 18%. How much interest did she pay for the month?

3. Hayley bought items costing $3.75, $8.22, $6.95, $4.43, and $6.95. What was the total amount of the purchases?

4. Reynard, star basketball player for Valley High, scored 25, 38, 18, 23, and 31 points in five consecutive games. What was his scoring average?

5. The seating capacity of Riverfront Stadium is 51,786. The stadium is $\frac{2}{3}$ full. How many people are in attendance?

Evaluating Information

For each problem, decide whether the information given is enough, not enough, or more than necessary to solve the problem. Circle the correct answer.

1. Maya bought a coat for $153.30 at a 30% off sale. What was the original price of the coat?

   a. enough   **b.** not enough   **c.** more than necessary

2. Angel drove his automobile 216 miles on Tuesday and averaged 45 miles per hour. On Friday his average rate was 38 miles per hour for the 375 miles that he drove. He used a total of 35 gallons of fuel for both days. How many miles per gallon did he average?

   a. enough   **b.** not enough   **c.** more than necessary

3. During the month of February, the Wilson family spent 20% of their food budget for fresh produce. The weekly amounts for fruit totaled $3.57, $2.92, $5.81, and $4.72. What total amount was spent for produce?

   a. enough   **b.** not enough   **c.** more than necessary

4. Eric has 5 wooden poles he is going to cut into pieces $10\frac{1}{2}$ inches long. How many such pieces can he get from each pole?

   a. enough   **b.** not enough   **c.** more than necessary

5. Linda's motorboat averages 4 miles per hour upstream and 6 miles per hour downstream when traveling on Shiney River. On a trip 24 miles upstream and back, the average rate was 4.8 miles per hour. How long did the trip take?

   a. enough   **b.** not enough   **c.** more than necessary

Word Problems

Solve each problem.

---

1. If $2,256 is divided equally among 47 people, how much will each person receive?

---

2. Tammer earned $3,268.62 interest on his investment of $72,636 in six months. What was the annual rate of interest?

---

3. Ricky Lee has a board 8 feet long. He cuts $5\frac{3}{4}$ feet off of it. What is the length of the board that is left?

---

4. Mr. Jones bought 7 cases of frozen orange juice with 48 cans in each case. How many cans of orange juice did he buy?

---

5. Normal rainfall in San Francisco is 19.53 inches. How much precipitation would there be in a year that had 90% of the normal rainfall amount?

Estimation

Circle the best estimate for the answer to each problem.

1. The number of students enrolled in each of seven high schools is 1,862, 1,543, 2,130, 965, 2,341, 1,156, and 1,432, respectively. What is the average number enrolled in each school?

    a. 1,600   **b.** 1,000   **c.** 2,000   **d.** 1,400

2. The Kelly Scholarship fund of $12,620 at Baker High is invested at 13% annual interest. What amount of interest is earned in one year?

    a. $1,000   **b.** $1,200   **c.** $1,600   **d.** $2,000

3. How many square feet of sod will it take to cover a rectangular plot with dimensions 1,263 feet by 982 feet?

    a. 1,000   **b.** 1,000,000   **c.** 10,000   **d.** 100,000

4. Marcel worked 4 hours 15 minutes on each of thirteen different days. What is the total number of hours that he worked?

    a. 65   **b.** 40   **c.** 55   **d.** 75

5. Mrs. Gluchowski bought 5 packages of ground beef weighing $4\frac{1}{4}$, $3\frac{5}{8}$, $2\frac{1}{2}$, $5\frac{3}{4}$, and $4\frac{3}{4}$ pounds, respectively. What was the total weight of the meat?

    a. 100 pounds   **b.** 15 pounds   **c.** 25 pounds   **d.** 20 pounds

Word Problems

Solve each problem.

---

1. Kelly has 52 customers on her paper route. She delivers 6 newspapers to each customer each week. How many newspapers is this in all?

---

2. Jenni, Joan, Jim, and Jamar took orders for Christmas carnations of 75, 86, 102, and 73, respectively. What was the average number of orders they took?

---

3. Priyanka earned $170.10 on her investment at 6.3% simple interest for two years. What amount did she have invested?

---

4. The cost of gasoline is $1.57 cents per gallon. What is the cost of 13 gallons?

---

5. Jackson turned in twelve homework papers with grades 10, 8, 8, 7, 5, 4, 3, 9, 6, 9, 6, and 9. What was the total of his homework grades?

Estimation

Circle the best estimate for the answer to each problem.

---

1. Find the volume, in gallons, of a rectangular box that is 2 feet long, 1 foot wide, and 3 feet tall. There are 7.48 gallons in a cubic foot.

   a. 500　　　　　**b.** 50　　　　　**c.** 10　　　　　**d.** 5

---

2. Find the perimeter of a rectangle with length 2.32 m and width 1.81 m.

   a. 12 m　　　　　**b.** 8 m　　　　　**c.** 6 m　　　　　**d.** 4 m

---

3. The attendance each night for the performance of the Super Band was 12,563, 10,291, 5,432, and 8,652. What was the total attendance for the four performances?

   a. 35,000　　　　　**b.** 37,000　　　　　**c.** 40,000　　　　　**d.** 42,000

---

4. In 1947, Jacquiline Cochran broke the international speed record for a piston-driven airplane over a 100 kilometer flight without payload by traveling 755.668 kilometers per hour. At this rate, how much time did it take to travel the 100 kilometers?

   a. 8 minutes　　　　　**b.** 30 minutes　　　　　**c.** 1 hour　　　　　**d.** 4 minutes

---

5. Willie Shoemaker, a jockey, won $1,329,890 in 1951, $1,784,187 in 1953, $1,876,760 in 1954, $2,961,693 in 1958, $2,843,133 in 1959, $2,123,961 in 1960, $2,690,819 in 1961, $2,916,844 in 1962, $2,526,925 in 1963, and $2,649,553 in 1964. What were his total winnings during those years?

   a. $10,000,000　　　　　**b.** $15,000,000　　　　　**c.** $25,000,000　　　　　**d.** $50,000,000

Word Problems

Solve each problem.

---

1. Vicky saved $63.35. She spent $28.50 on a new dress. How much did she have left?

---

2. Randy took 9 weekly tests during the first quarter of the second semester. His grades were 100, 85, 72, 62, 92, 67, 80, 76, and 95. Find the average of his test grades.

---

3. Mr. Summerville borrowed $27,000 for one year at 8% simple interest. What was the amount of interest he paid?

---

4. Pedro answered 32 problems correctly on a 40-problem test. What percent of the problems did he answer correctly?

---

5. Carol needs four pieces of lumber, one $6\frac{1}{2}$ feet long, two $3\frac{3}{4}$ feet long, and one $5\frac{1}{4}$ feet long. What is the total length she needs?

Estimation

Circle the best estimate for the answer to each problem.

1. The estimated per-pupil expenditure in the U.S. public schools was $1,281 during the 1973–74 school year. The average daily attendance was 42,079,000. What was the total amount spent for public schools during that year?

   a. $5,000,000   **b.** $50,000,000   **c.** $50,000,000,000   **d.** $500,000,000

2. The ten tallest buildings in New York City have heights of 1,350 feet, 1,250 feet, 1,046 feet, 950 feet, 927 feet, 900 feet, 850 feet, 813 feet, 808 feet, and 792 feet. What is the average height of these buildings?

   a. 1,320 feet   **b.** 810 feet   **c.** 1,580 feet   **d.** 970 feet

3. How much money must be invested at $12\frac{1}{2}\%$ per year to earn $5,000 in one year?

   a. $40,000   **b.** $50,000   **c.** $70,000   **d.** $100,000

4. A cylindrical water container is 18 inches in diameter and 24 inches tall. What is the volume of the container in cubic inches?

   a. 2,000   **b.** 6,000   **c.** 10,000   **d.** 15,000

5. Normal body temperature is 98.6°F. What is normal body temperature when measured in degrees Celsius?

   a. 72   **b.** 120   **c.** 37   **d.** 235

Word Problems

Solve each problem.

---

1. Mary Ann drove 672 miles in 16 hours. How many miles per hour did she average?

---

2. From March 1, how many days are there until the end of school on June 15? (Note: There are 31 days in March, 30 days in April, and 31 days in May.)

---

3. Jerry bought $3\frac{5}{8}$ ounces of caramel, $6\frac{3}{4}$ ounces of mints, and $7\frac{1}{2}$ ounces of brittle in the candy store. How many ounces of candy did he buy in all?

---

4. Octavius paid $910.16 interest on $3,670 he borrowed at 6.2% simple interest. For what length of time was the money borrowed?

---

5. Kyra spent $18.75 of her $25 allowance to buy a compact disc. How much money did she have left?

Estimation

Circle the best estimate for the answer to each problem.

1. In 1976, the University of California at Berkeley had 29,730 students and 2,384 teachers. What was the ratio of students to teachers?

   a. 12 to 1   **b.** 25 to 1   **c.** 35 to 1   **d.** 50 to 1

2. A train traveled 2,210 miles at an average rate of 59 miles per hour. How many hours did the trip take?

   a. 22   **b.** 37   **c.** 49   **d.** 41

3. A square plot of land is 1 mile long and 1 mile wide. Jill jogged all the way around the perimeter of the plot. How many yards did she jog?

   a. 21,000   **b.** 7,000   **c.** 2,100   **d.** 700

4. It is $60\frac{1}{2}$ feet from the pitcher's mound to home plate on a baseball diamond. The pitcher throws the ball so that it travels at an average rate of 90 miles per hour. How long will it take the ball to reach home plate?

   a. 0.5 second   **b.** 2 seconds   **c.** 0.2 second   **d.** 1.5 seconds

5. An irrigation sprinkler can water a circular area that has a radius of 120 feet. How many square yards can be watered by this sprinkler?

   a. 45,000   **b.** 4,500   **c.** 500   **d.** 5,000

Word Problems

Solve each problem.

1. Two hundred fifty-six people have been invited to a reception. Sixty-eight people have called to say they cannot attend. How many guests should be expected?

2. Mr. Phillips has to pay a 5% penalty because his payment of $170 was late. What is the amount of the penalty he has to pay?

3. Ms. Khoklova borrowed $4,732 at simple interest for two years and paid $1,135.68 in interest. What was the rate of interest?

4. On a 1,365 mile trip, Nance averaged 18.2 miles per gallon of gasoline. How many gallons of gasoline did she use?

5. If the cost of gasoline is $1.65 cents per gallon, what is the cost of 13.2 gallons?

Estimation

Circle the best estimate for the answer to each problem.

1. Mr. Tallfeather invested some money at 15% annual interest. He earned $3,570 in a two-year period. How much money did he have invested at this rate?

   a. $24,000   **b.** $2,400   **c.** $120,000   **d.** $12,000

2. The circular top and bottom of an oil drum are 24 inches in diameter. The drum is 40 inches high. What is the volume of the drum?

   a. 10 ft^3 **b.** 8 ft^3 **c.** 18,000 in^3 **d.** 2 yd^3

3. Sixty-one degrees Fahrenheit is how many degrees Celsius?

   a. 140   **b.** 15   **c.** 3   **d.** 67

4. Rob used 22 boards, each $6\frac{1}{4}$ feet long; 10 boards, each $10\frac{2}{3}$ feet long; 18 boards, each $1\frac{1}{4}$ feet long; and 6 boards, each $3\frac{3}{4}$ feet long to build a storage shed. What was the total length (in feet) of boards used to construct the shed?

   a. 290   **b.** 22   **c.** 56   **d.** 152

5. A farm-equipment dealer sold 252 tractors for a total of $8,756,000. What was the average price of each tractor?

   a. $3,500   **b.** $25,000   **c.** $35,000   **d.** $2,500

Answers to Exercises

PAGE 4
1. 9, 11, 13, 15, 17, 19, 21, 23, 25, 27, 29, 31 **2.** 10, 12, 14, 16, 18, 20, 22, 24, 26, 28, 30, 32 **3.** 14, 17, 20, 23, 26, 29, 32, 35, 38, 41, 44, 47 **4.** 17, 21, 25, 29, 33, 37, 41, 45, 49, 53, 57, 61 **5.** 50, 60, 70, 80, 90, 100, 110, 120, 130, 140, 150, 160 **6.** 25, 36, 49, 64, 81, 100, 121, 144, 169, 196, 225, 256 **7.** 26, 37, 50, 65, 82, 101, 122, 145, 170, 197, 226, 257 **8.** 15, 21, 28, 36, 45, 55, 66, 78, 91, 105, 120, 136 **9.** 81, 243, 729, 2,187, 6,561, 19,683, 59,049, 177,147, 531,441, 1,594,323 **10.** 13, 21, 34, 55, 89, 144, 233, 377, 610, 987

PAGE 5
1. 22 **2.** 55 **3.** 306 **4.** 319 **5.** 140 **6.** 264 **7.** 89 **8.** $1,176 **9.** 165 **10.** 23 in.

PAGE 6
1. 25, 30, 35, 40, 45, 50, 55, 60, 65, 70, 75, 80 **2.** 30, 36, 42, 48, 54, 60, 66, 72, 78, 84, 90, 96 **3.** 25, 31, 37, 43, 49, 55, 61, 67, 73, 79, 85, 91 **4.** 34, 42, 50, 58, 66, 74, 82, 90, 98, 106, 114, 122 **5.** 26, 31, 36, 41, 46, 51, 56, 61, 66, 71, 76, 81 **6.** 24, 35, 48, 63, 80, 99, 120, 143, 168, 195, 224, 255 **7.** 126, 217, 344, 513, 730, 1,001, 1,332, 1,729, 2,198, 2,745, 3,376, 4,097 **8.** 11, 16, 22, 29, 37, 46, 56, 67, 79, 92, 106, 121 **9.** 512, 256, 128, 64, 32, 16, 8, 4, 2, 1 **10.** 7, 32, 9, 64, 11, 128, 13, 256, 15, 512

PAGE 7
1. 31 **2.** 49 **3.** 331 **4.** 414 **5.** 152 **6.** 256 **7.** 85 **8.** $1,157 **9.** 162 **10.** 20 in.

PAGE 8
1. 15, 18, 21, 24, 27, 30, 33, 36, 39, 42, 45, 48 **2.** 45, 54, 63, 72, 81, 90, 99, 108, 117, 126, 135, 144 **3.** 35, 43, 51, 59, 67, 75, 83, 91, 99, 107, 115, 123 **4.** 21, 25, 29, 33, 37, 41, 45, 49, 53, 57, 61, 65 **5.** 48, 58, 68, 78, 88, 98, 108, 118, 128, 138, 148, 158 **6.** 16, 32, 64, 128, 256, 512, 1,024, 2,048, 4,096, 8,192, 16,384, 32,768 **7.** 17, 33, 65, 129, 257, 513, 1,025, 2,049, 4,097, 8,193, 16,385, 32,769 **8.** 19, 26, 34, 43, 53, 64, 76, 89, 103, 118, 134, 151 **9.** 17, 26, 37, 50, 65, 82, 101, 122, 145, 170 **10.** 7, 6, 8, 7, 9, 8, 10, 9, 11, 10

PAGE 9
1. 72 **2.** 50 **3.** 498 **4.** 878 **5.** 160 **6.** 241 **7.** 85 **8.** $1,065 **9.** 140 **10.** 25 in.

PAGE 10
1. 40, 48, 56, 64, 72, 80, 88, 96, 104, 112, 120, 128 **2.** 20, 24, 28, 32, 36, 40, 44, 48, 52, 56, 60, 64 **3.** 42, 51, 60, 69, 78, 87, 96, 105, 114, 123, 132, 141 **4.** 39, 48, 57, 66, 75, 84, 93, 102, 111, 120, 129, 138 **5.** 47, 57, 67, 77, 87, 97, 107, 117, 127, 137, 147, 157 **6.** 27, 38, 51, 66, 83, 102, 123, 146, 171, 198, 227, 258 **7.** 125, 216, 343, 512, 729, 1,000, 1,331, 1,728, 2,197, 2,744, 3,375, 4,096 **8.** 21, 31, 43, 57, 73, 91, 111, 133, 157, 183, 211, 241 **9.** 16, 22, 29, 37, 46, 56, 67, 79, 92, 106, 121, 137 **10.** 25, 12, 30, 14, 35, 16, 40, 18, 45, 20

PAGE 11
1. 51 **2.** 83 **3.** 575 **4.** 826 **5.** 134 **6.** 291 **7.** 83 **8.** $1,069 **9.** 157 **10.** 21 in.

PAGE 12
1. 35, 42, 49, 56, 63, 70, 77, 84, 91, 98, 105, 112 **2.** 55, 66, 77, 88, 99, 110, 121, 132, 143, 154, 165, 176 **3.** 32, 39, 46, 53, 60, 67, 74, 81, 88, 95, 102, 109 **4.** 28, 33, 38, 43, 48, 53, 58, 63, 68, 73, 78, 83 **5.** 46, 56, 66, 76, 86, 96, 106, 116, 126, 136, 146, 156 **6.** 18, 34, 66, 130, 258, 514, 1,026, 2,050, 4,098, 8,194, 16,386, 32,770 **7.** 128, 219, 346, 515, 732, 1,003, 1,334, 1,731, 2,200, 2,747, 3,378, 4,099 **8.** 14, 20, 27, 35, 44, 54, 65, 77, 90, 104, 119, 135 **9.** 16, 19, 22, 25, 28, 31, 34, 37, 40, 43, 46, 49 **10.** 16, 25, 32, 36, 64, 49, 128, 64, 256, 81, 512, 100

PAGE 13
1. 55 **2.** 42 **3.** 438 **4.** 661 **5.** 125 **6.** 237 **7.** 85 **8.** $1,099 **9.** 159 **10.** 26 in.

PAGE 14
1. $4,886 **2.** $5,524 **3.** $5,194 **4.** $5,666 **5.** $5,014 **6.** $5,966 **7.** $6,019 **8.** $5,269 **9.** $5,704 **10.** $5,884 **11.** $1,283 **12.** $1,303 **13.** $1,658 **14.** $1,493 **15.** $1,563 **16.** $1,863 **17.** $1,748 **18.** $2,243 **19.** $1,998 **20.** $2,183 **21.** $2.62 **22.** $2.08 **23.** $2.80 **24.** $1.68 **25.** $1.72 **26.** $3.13 **27.** $2.50 **28.** $2.01 **29.** $3.22 **30.** $1.95

PAGE 15
1. 361 **2.** 3,844 **3.** 961 **4.** 5,625 **5.** 9 **6.** 14,400 **7.** 18,496 **8.** 7,225 **9.** 22,500 **10.** 2,025 **11.** 1.732 **12.** 5.196 **13.** 10.149 **14.** 9.165 **15.** 4.796 **16.** 9.747 **17.** 10.050 **18.** 7.141 **19.** 8.944 **20.** 5.292 **21.** 35 **22.** 5 **23.** 73 **24.** 25 **25.** 89 **26.** 16 **27.** 55 **28.** 99 **29.** 64 **30.** 45

PAGE 16
1. $4,969 **2.** $5,936 **3.** $5,381 **4.** $5,149 **5.** $5,689 **6.** $4,834 **7.** $6,094 **8.** $5,524 **9.** $5,801 **10.** $5,269 **11.** $1,333 **12.** $1,513 **13.** $1,643 **14.** $2,058 **15.** $2,473 **16.** $2,268 **17.** $1,713 **18.** $1,368 **19.** $2,143 **20.** $1,688 **21.** $2.45 **22.** $1.74 **23.** $2.57 **24.** $3.20 **25.** $2.12 **26.** $3.07 **27.** $2.72 **28.** $1.83 **29.** $1.65 **30.** $2.20

PAGE 17
1. 2,500 **2.** 49 **3.** 8,281 **4.** 4,225 **5.** 15,129 **6.** 6,084 **7.** 400 **8.** 19,600 **9.** 13,456 **10.** 1,156 **11.** 7.348 **12.** 8.660 **13.** 2.236 **14.** 6.782 **15.** 10.954 **16.** 10.677 **17.** 5.196 **18.** 9.327 **19.** 7.937 **20.** 10.440 **21.** 57 **22.** 17 **23.** 47 **24.** 75 **25.** 91 **26.** 7 **27.** 108 **28.** 76 **29.** 27 **30.** 37

PAGE 18
1. $6,064 **2.** $4,909 **3.** $5,201 **4.** $5,584 **5.** $5,981 **6.** $5,546 **7.** $5,801 **8.** $4,999 **9.** $5,396 **10.** $6,146 **11.** $2,433 **12.** $1,968 **13.** $2,038 **14.** $1,623 **15.** $1,493 **16.** $1,548 **17.** $2,148 **18.** $1,523 **19.** $1,673 **20.** $1,913 **21.** $2.52 **22.** $2.24 **23.** $1.91 **24.** $2.83 **25.** $2.72 **26.** $1.66 **27.** $1.80 **28.** $3.27 **29.** $1.99 **30.** $2.98

PAGE 19
1. 15,376 **2.** 529 **3.** 20,164 **4.** 1,444 **5.** 11,664 **6.** 6,561 **7.** 100
8. 2,809 **9.** 10,609 **10.** 4,624 **11.** 8,426 **12.** 11.180 **13.** 2.646
14. 12.247 **15.** 9.592 **16.** 5.477 **17.** 11.832 **18.** 8.944
19. 10.770 **20.** 9.220 **21.** 29 **22.** 9 **23.** 104 **24.** 39 **25.** 93
26. 19 **27.** 110 **28.** 59 **29.** 106 **30.** 49

PAGE 20
1. $4,924 **2.** $6,004 **3.** $5,254 **4.** $5,059 **5.** $5,906 **6.** $5,171
7. $5,839 **8.** $5,509 **9.** $6,139 **10.** $5,606 **11.** $1,543 **12.** $1,498
13. $2,068 **14.** $2,023 **15.** $1,623 **16.** $2,353 **17.** $2,153
18. $1,478 **19.** $2,218 **20.** $1,583 **21.** $1.84 **22.** $2.07
23. $1.75 **24.** $2.62 **25.** $2.36 **26.** $2.20 **27.** $3.17 **28.** $3.01
29. $2.91 **30.** $1.92

PAGE 21
1. 4,900 **2.** 169 **3.** 12,544 **4.** 3,249 **5.** 16,900 **6.** 625 **7.** 11,664
8. 6,724 **9.** 5,776 **10.** 1,600 **11.** 5.916 **12.** 9.220 **13.** 2.828
14. 11.533 **15.** 7.874 **16.** 8.544 **17.** 10.677 **18.** 7.348
19. 11.225 **20.** 3.464 **21.** 41 **22.** 21 **23.** 102 **24.** 51 **25.** 112
26. 31 **27.** 61 **28.** 11 **29.** 95 **30.** 66

PAGE 22
1. $5,066 **2** $5,224 **3.** $5,869 **4.** $5,569 **5.** $5,306 **6.** $4,886
7. $5,846 **8.** $5,576 **9.** $5,471 **10.** $5,974 **11.** $2,128 **12.** $2,108
13. $1,978 **14.** $1,688 **15.** $1,573 **16.** $1,503 **17.** $1,338
18. $2,478 **19.** $1,548 **20.** $2,158 **21.** $3.11 **22.** $2.27
23. $1.91 **24.** $2.87 **25.** $2.04 **26.** $1.79 **27.** $2.46 **28.** $2.69
29. $3.24 **30.** $2.17

PAGE 23
1. 15,625 **2.** 841 **3.** 9,604 **4.** 5,476 **5.** 13,225 **6.** 256 **7.** 17,424
8. 1,849 **9.** 18,225 **10.** 3,600 **11.** 9.798 **12.** 6.782 **13.** 10.149
14. 12.166 **15.** 4.123 **16.** 11.533 **17.** 9.055 **18.** 8.185 **19.** 7.416
20. 4.359 **21.** 33 **22.** 97 **23.** 43 **24.** 116 **25.** 14 **26.** 62 **27.** 100
28. 23 **29.** 30 **30.** 53

Answers for pages 28–37 are actual data figures. Students' answers
may vary.

PAGE 29
1.a. $0.57 **b.** $1.22 **c.** $1.20 **d.** $1.22 **e.** $1.20 **f.** $1.17 **g.** $1.21
h. $1.29 **2.a.** $110 **b.** $114 **c.** $118 **d.** $124 **e.** $131 **f.** $136
g. $140 **h.** $145 **i.** $148 **j.** $152 **k.** $157 **l.** $161

PAGE 30
1. a. 6.2% **b.** 6.2% **c.** 6.2% **d.** 6.4% **e.** 6.4% **f.** 6.4% **g.** 7.0%
h. 7.2% **i.** 7.6% **2. a.** 10% **b.** 8.5% **c.** 8.0% **d.** 7.5% **e.** 6.0%
f. 6.0% **g.** 6.5% **h.** 7.0% **i.** 5.5% **j.** 3.0% **k.** 3.5% **l.** 4.75%

PAGE 31
1. a. 4 in. **b.** 4.5 in. **c.** 5 in. **d.** 3.5 in. **e.** 3.5 in. **f.** 4 in. **g.** 6 in.
h. 5.5 in. **i.** 4 in. **j.** 3 in. **k.** 3 in. **l.** 4 in. **2. a.** 2.5 in. **b.** 2 in.
c. 3 in. **d.** 3 in. **e.** 3.5 in. **f.** 4 in. **g.** 3.5 in. **h.** 3 in. **i.** 2.5 in.
j. 2 in. **k.** 2.5 in. **l.** 3 in.

PAGE 32
1. a. 40°F **b.** 45°F **c.** 50°F **d.** 60°F **e.** 65°F **f.** 75°F **g.** 85°F
h. 85°F **i.** 75°F **j.** 60°F **k.** 45°F **l.** 40°F **2. a.** 40°F **b.** 45°F **c.** 50°F
d. 55°F **e.** 60°F **f.** 65°F **g.** 70°F **h.** 65°F **i.** 60°F **j.** 55°F **k.** 50°F
l. 45°F

PAGE 33
1. a. 35% **b.** $42\frac{1}{2}$% **c.** 45% **d.** $32\frac{1}{2}$% **e.** $37\frac{1}{2}$% **f.** 40%
g. $42\frac{1}{2}$% **h.** 44% **i.** 45% **j.** 45% **k.** $42\frac{1}{2}$% **l.** 35% **m.** $32\frac{1}{2}$%
2. a. 6.5% **b.** 6.1% **c.** 6.2% **d.** 6.0% **e.** 6.1% **f.** 5.7% **g.** 6.2%
h. 5.9% **i.** 6.0% **j.** 5.8% **k.** 5.8% **l.** 5.9%

PAGE 34
1. a. 6.7 million **b.** 6.2 million **c.** 6.5 million **d.** 6.4 million
e. 6.4 million **f.** 8.0 million **g.** 6.0 million **h.** 6.3 million
2. a. 12.5 million **b.** 37.5 million **c.** 43 million **d.** 15 million
e. 31 million **f.** 12.5 million **g.** 19 million **h.** 8 million
i. 27.5 million

PAGE 35
1. a. $393 billion **b.** $400 billion **c.** $402 billion **d.** $404 billion
e. $410 billion **f.** $414 billion **g.** $415 billion **h.** $421 billion
2. a. 1,420 thousand **b.** 2,020 thousand **c.** 2,380 thousand
d. 2,020 thousand **e.** 1,380 thousand **f.** 1,180 thousand
g. 1,590 thousand **h.** 2,000 thousand **i.** 2,100 thousand
j. 1,100 thousand **k.** 1,200 thousand

PAGE 36
1. a. $1,060,000 **b.** $1,170,000 **c.** $420,000 **d.** $540,000
e. $260,000 **f.** $390,000 **g.** $260,000 **h.** $380,000
2. a. 9.9 million **b.** 8.8 million **c.** 9.7 million **d.** 10.9 million
e. 12.3 million **f.** 12.0 million **g.** 11.8 million

PAGE 37
1. a. 25 million **b.** 27.5 million **c.** 32.5 million **d.** 30 million
e. 32 million **f.** 44 million **g.** 52.5 million **h.** 42.5 million
i. 50 million **2. a.** 12.5 million **b.** 16 million **c.** 22.5 million
d. 23.5 million **e.** 25 million **f.** 32.5 million **g.** 42.5 million
h. 37.5 million **i.** 42 million

PAGE 38
1. a. 500,000 **b.** 700,000 **c.** 850,000 **d.** 900,000 **e.** 950,000
f. 1,250,000 **g.** 2,000,000 **h.** 1,700,000 **i.** 2,500,000 **2. a.** $1,000
b. $1,000 **c.** $1,500 **d.** $1,500 **e.** $3,000 **f.** $5,000 **g.** $9,500
h. $12,000 **i.** $28,500

PAGE 39
1. **Percent Change in Consumer Price Index**

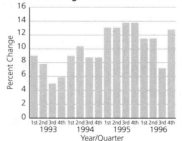

Basic Computation Series 2000: Applying Computational Skills
ANSWERS TO EXERCISES

2.

Average Prime Interest Rate

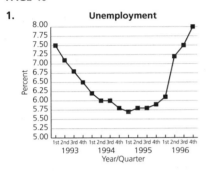

PAGE 40

1.

Unemployment

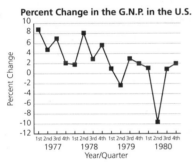

2.

Percent Change in the G.N.P. in the U.S.

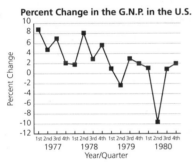

PAGE 41

1.

Net Sales

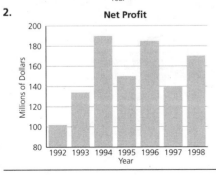

2.

Net Profit

Average Amount of Daylight

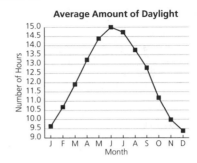

PAGE 43

1.

Leading Causes of Death

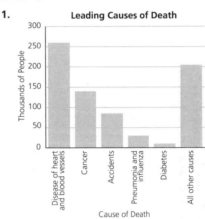

2.

Male Life Expectancy at Birth

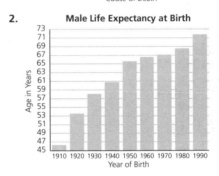

PAGE 44

1.

Female Life Expectancy at Birth

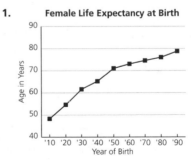

2.

Births in the U.S.

PAGE 45

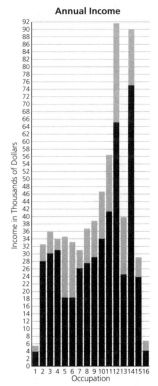

Annual Income

PAGE 46

1.

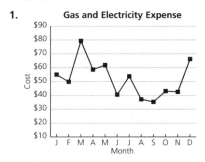

Gas and Electricity Expense

2.

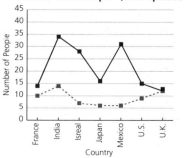

Birthrate/Deathrate per 1,000 Population

PAGE 47

1.

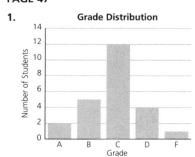

Grade Distribution

2.

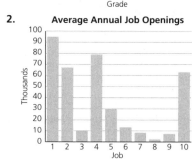

Average Annual Job Openings

PAGE 48

1.

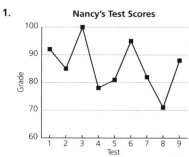

Nancy's Test Scores

2.

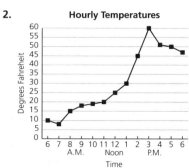

Hourly Temperatures

Basic Computation Series 2000: Applying Computational Skills
ANSWERS TO EXERCISES

PAGE 49

1. a. $22,500 **b.** $17,250 **c.** $13,500 **d.** $3,000 **e.** $8,250
f. $5,250 **g.** $3,000 **h.** $2,250 **2. a.** $15,318 **b.** $3,108 **c.** $6,660
d. $9,324 **e.** $888 **f.** $1,332 **g.** $4,218 **h.** $3,552

PAGE 50

1. **Wheat and Coarse Grain Production**

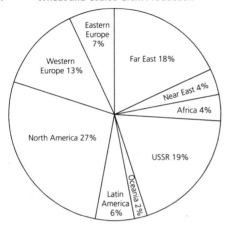

2. **Grade Points**

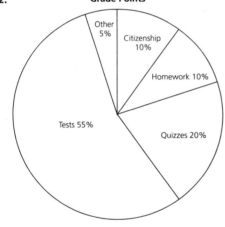

PAGE 51

1. a. $258,000,000,000 **b.** $180,000,000,000 **c.** $78,000,000,000
d. $24,000,000,000 **e.** $30,000,000,000 **f.** $30,000,000,000
2. a. $1,100 **b.** $800 **c.** $600 **d.** $1,000 **e.** $850 **f.** $450 **g.** $200

PAGE 52

1. **Federal Expenditures (out of each dollar)**

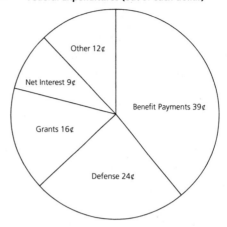

2. **Family Expenditures (out of each dollar)**

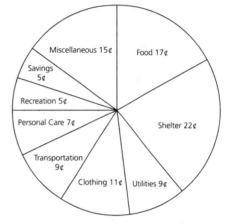

PAGE 53

1. a. $93,120,000 **b.** $38,800,000 **c.** $166,840,000 **d.** $46,560,000
e. $42,680,000 **2. a.** $201,720,000 **b.** $113,160,000 **c.** $59,040,000
d. $9,840,000 **e.** $108,240,000

PAGE 54

1. **Sales**

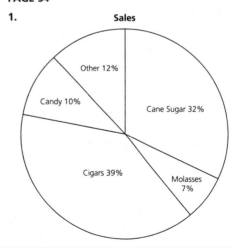

2. Sales

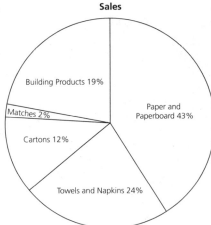

- Building Products 19%
- Matches 2%
- Cartons 12%
- Towels and Napkins 24%
- Paper and Paperboard 43%

2. Oil Imports

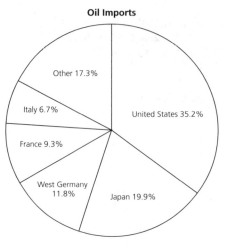

- Other 17.3%
- Italy 6.7%
- France 9.3%
- West Germany 11.8%
- Japan 19.9%
- United States 35.2%

PAGE 55

1. a. $12,000,000 **b.** $8,000,000 **c.** $2,200,000 **d.** $1,600,000
e. $3,800,000 **f.** $2,000,000 **g.** $2,000,000 **h.** $400,000
2. a. $35,100,000,000 **b.** $9,750,000,000 **c.** $9,490,000,000
d. $8,580,000,000 **e.** $7,670,000,000 **f.** $6,500,000,000

PAGE 56

1. Choice Beef: Income and Expenses

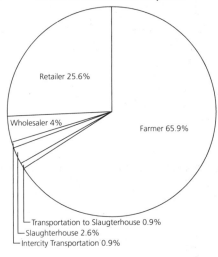

- Retailer 25.6%
- Wholesaler 4%
- Farmer 65.9%
- Transportation to Slaugterhouse 0.9%
- Slaughterhouse 2.6%
- Intercity Transportation 0.9%

PAGE 57

1. a. 40,280 **b.** 33,920 **c.** 27,560 **d.** 22,260 **e.** 21,200 **f.** 16,960
g. 49,820 **2. a.** 210,000 **b.** 200,000 **c.** 180,000 **d.** 130,000
e. 64,000 **f.** 56,000 **g.** 160,000

PAGE 58

1. Workers in New York

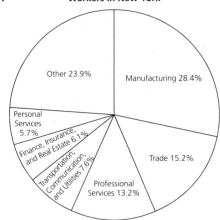

- Other 23.9%
- Manufacturing 28.4%
- Personal Services 5.7%
- Finance, Insurance, and Real Estate 6.1%
- Transportation, Communication, and Utilities 7.6%
- Trade 15.2%
- Professional Services 13.2%

2. Workers in Texas

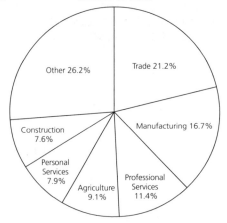

- Other 26.2%
- Trade 21.2%
- Construction 7.6%
- Manufacturing 16.7%
- Personal Services 7.9%
- Agriculture 9.1%
- Professional Services 11.4%

For pages 58–67, answers 10% higher or lower than the distances given are acceptable.

PAGE 59
1. 29 mm, 72.5 km **2.** 38 mm, 95.0 km **3.** 124 mm, 310.0 km
4. 56 mm, 140.0 km **5.** 44 mm, 110.0 km

PAGE 60
1. 73 mm, 182.5 km **2.** 87 mm, 217.5 km **3.** 71 mm, 177.5 km
4. 114 mm, 285.0 km **5.** 137 mm, 342.5 km

PAGE 61
1. 32 mm, 80.0 km **2.** 48 mm, 120.0 km **3.** 77 mm, 192.5 km
4. 88 mm, 220.0 km **5.** 55 mm, 137.5 km

PAGE 62
1. 93 mm, 232.5 km **2.** 83 mm, 207.5 km **3.** 109 mm, 272.5 km
4. 80 mm, 200.0 km **5.** 114 mm, 285.0 km

PAGE 63
1. 38 mm, 95.0 km **2.** 60 mm, 150.0 km **3.** 97 mm, 242.5 km
4. 97 mm, 242.5 km **5.** 95 mm, 237.5 km

PAGE 64
1. 134 mm, 335.0 km **2.** 124 mm, 310.0 km **3.** 134 mm,
335.0 km **4.** 59 mm, 147.5 km **5.** 163 mm, 407.5 km

PAGE 65
1. 39 mm, 97.5 km **2.** 60 mm, 150.0 km **3.** 109 mm, 272.5 km
4. 118 mm, 295.0 km **5.** 82 mm, 205.0 km

PAGE 66
1. 109 mm, 272.5 km **2.** 112 mm, 280.0 km **3.** 159 mm, 397.5 km
4. 118 mm, 295.0 km **5.** 138 mm, 345.0 km

PAGE 67
1. 57 mm, 142.5 km **2.** 77 mm, 192.5 km **3.** 105 mm, 262.5 km
4. 109 mm, 272.5 km **5.** 58 mm, 145.0 km

PAGE 68
1. 111 mm, 277.5 km **2.** 112 mm, 280.0 km **3.** 131 mm, 327.5 km
4. 144 mm, 360.0 km **5.** 111 mm, 277.5 km

PAGE 71
1. $15.69; 1 $10 bill, 1 $5 bill, 2 quarters, 1 dime, 1 nickel,
4 pennies **2.** $5.69; 1 $5 bill, 2 quarters, 1 dime, 1 nickel, 4 pennies
3. $0.69; 2 quarters, 1 dime, 1 nickel, 4 pennies **4.** $1.04; 1 $1 bill,
4 pennies **5.** $0.19; 1 dime, 1 nickel, 4 pennies **6.** $12.43;
1 $10 bill, 2 $1 bills 1 quarter, 1 dime, 1 nickel, 3 pennies **7.** $2.43;
2 $1 bills, 1 quarter, 1 dime, 1 nickel, 3 pennies **8.** $5.00; 1 $5 bill
9. $3.03; 3 $1 bills, 3 pennies **10.** $0.43; 1 quarter, 1 dime, 1 nickel,
3 pennies

PAGE 72
1. a. 0.5¢ each **b.** 0.4¢ each **c.** 0.3 ¢ each (best buy)
2. a. 16.3¢ per oz (best buy) **b.** 19.8¢ per oz **c.** 17.0¢ per oz
3. a. 6.7¢ per oz **b.** 5.0¢ per oz (best buy) **c.** 5.7¢ per oz
4. a. 4.3¢ per oz **b.** 4.7¢ per oz **c.** 4.2¢ per oz (best buy)
5. a. 4.3¢ per oz (best buy) **b.** 4.5¢ per oz **c.** 4.6¢ per oz
6. a. 12.7¢ per oz **b.** 12.1¢ per oz (best buy) **c.** 12.6¢ per oz
7. a. 12.4¢ per oz **b.** 11.3¢ per oz (best buy) **c.** 11.5¢ per oz
8. a. 4.1¢ per oz **b.** 3.6¢ per oz **c.** 3.4¢ per oz (best buy)
9. a. 3.1¢ per oz **b.** 2.9¢ per oz (best buy) **c.** 3.0¢ per oz
10. a. 0.8¢ per ft **b.** 0.6¢ per ft **c.** 0.5¢ per ft (best buy)

PAGE 73
1. $5.83; 1 $5 bill, 3 quarters, 1 nickel, 3 pennies **2.** $1.08; 1 $1 bill,
1 nickel, 3 pennies **3.** $1.00; 1 $1 bill **4.** $0.83; 3 quarters, 1 nickel,
3 pennies **5.** $45.25; 4 $10 bills, 1 $5 bill, 1 quarter **6.** $7.47;
1 $5 bill, 2 $1 bills, 1 quarter, 2 dimes, 2 pennies **7.** $8.00; 1 $5 bill,
3 $1 bills **8.** $2.47; 2 $1 bills, 1 quarter, 2 dimes, 2 pennies
9. $2.52; 2 $1 bills, 2 quarters, 2 pennies **10.** $0.47; 1 quarter,
2 dimes, 2 pennies

PAGE 74
1. a. 3.8¢ per oz **b.** 3.3¢ per oz **c.** 2.4¢ per oz (best buy)
2. a. 11.9¢ each **b.** 10.0¢ each **c.** 7.5¢ each (best buy)
3. a. 66.5¢ per oz (best buy) **b.** 69.9¢ per oz **c.** 66.6¢ per oz
4. a. 1.8¢ each **b.** 1.5¢ each **c.** 1.4¢ each (best buy)
5. a. 32.3¢ per oz **b.** 33.2¢ per oz **c.** 23.3¢ per oz (best buy)
6. a. 1.0¢ each (best buy) **b.** 1.3¢ each **c.** 1.2¢ each
7. a. 12.4¢ per mL **b.** 11.3¢ per mL (best buy) **c.** 12.7¢ per mL
8. a. 5.7¢ each **b.** 4.0¢ each (best buy) **c.** 4.6¢ each
9. a. 5.9¢ per oz **b.** 5.3¢ per oz (best buy) **c.** 5.5¢ per oz
10. a. 2.5¢ per ft^2 (best buy) **b.** 3.1¢ per ft^2 **c.** 2.9¢ per ft^2

PAGE 75
1. $45.62; 4 $10 bills, 1 $ 5 bill, 2 quarters, 1 dime, 2 pennies
2. $15.62; 1 $10 bill, 1 $5 bill, 2 quarters. 1 dime, 2 pennies
3. $21.37; 2 $10 bills, 1 $1 bill, 1 quarter, 1 dime, 2 pennies
4. $0.62; 2 quarters, 1 dime, 2 pennies **5.** $6.12; 1 $5 bill, 1 $1 bill,
1 dime, 2 pennies **6.** $32.61; 3 $10 bills, 2 $1 bills, 2 quarters,
1 dime, 1 penny **7.** $19.86; 1 $10 bill, 1 $5 bill, 4 $1 bills,
3 quarters, 1 dime, 1 penny **8.** $13.11; 1 $10 bill, 3 $1 bills, 1 dime
1 penny **9.** $4.01; 4 $1 bills, 1 penny **10.** $0.11; 1 dime, 1 penny

PAGE 76
1. a. 0.6¢ each **b.** 0.4¢ each **c.** 0.2¢ each (best buy)
2. a. 22.7¢ per oz **b.** 21.0¢ per oz **c.** 18.6¢ per oz (best buy)
3. a. 6.0¢ per oz (best buy) **b.** 6.4¢ per oz **c.** 8.4¢ per oz
4. a. 5.6¢ per oz **b.** 4.0¢ per oz **c.** 3.7¢ per oz (best buy)
5. a. 4.2¢ per oz (best buy) **b.** 4.7¢ per oz **c.** 4.8¢ per oz
6. a. 14.1¢ per oz **b.** 13.2¢ per oz (best buy) **c.** 15.4¢ per oz
7. a. 11.6¢ per oz **b.** 10.3¢ per oz (best buy) **c.** 12.0¢ per oz
8. a. 3.8¢ per oz **b.** 3.4¢ per oz **c.** 3.1¢ per oz (best buy)
9. a. 2.4¢ per oz (best buy) **b.** 3.3¢ per oz **c.** 5.0¢ per oz
10. a. 0.4¢ per ft (best buy) **b.** 0.5¢ per ft **c.** 0.6¢ per ft

PAGE 77

1. $33.29; 3 $10 bills, 3 $1 bills, 1 quarter, 4 pennies **2.** $15.79; 1 $10 bill, 1 $5 bill, 3 quarters, 4 pennies **3.** $4.04; 4 $1 bills, 4 pennies **4.** $0.29; 1 quarter, 4 pennies **5.** $3.29; 3 $1 bills, 1 quarter, 4 pennies **6.** $115.58; 11 $10 bills, 1 $5 bill, 2 quarters, 1 nickel, 3 pennies **7.** $38.78; 3 $10 bills, 1 $5 bill, 3 $1 bills, 3 quarters, 3 pennies **8.** $23.78; 2 $10 bills, 3 $1 bills, 3 quarters, 3 pennies **9.** $4.03; 4 $1 bills, 3 pennies **10.** $1.28; 1 $1 bill, 1 quarter, 3 pennies

PAGE 78

1. a. 8.0¢ per oz **b.** 5.3¢ per oz **c.** 3.1¢ per oz (best buy)
2. a. 9.0¢ each **b.** 10.0¢ each **c.** 7.5¢ each (best buy)
3. a. 81.5¢ per oz **b.** 79.9¢ per oz (best buy) **c.** 87.5¢ per oz
4. a. 2.8¢ each **b.** 2.1¢ each **c.** 1.4¢ each (best buy)
5. a. 37.3¢ per oz **b.** 29.8¢ per oz **c.** 24.1¢ per oz (best buy)
6. a. 1.3¢ each **b.** 1.2¢ each (best buy) **c.** 1.4¢ each
7. a. 14.6¢ per mL **b.** 12.6¢ per mL (best buy) **c.** 14.9¢ per mL
8. a. 6.0¢ each **b.** 4.0¢ each (best buy) **c.** 4.5¢ each
9. a. 6.9¢ per oz **b.** 5.9¢ per oz (best buy) **c.** 6.0¢ per oz
10. a. 3.2¢ per ft^2 **b.** 3.5¢ per ft^2 **c.** 2.9¢ per ft^2 (best buy)

PAGE 79

1. $16.25; 1 $10 bill, 1 $5 bill, 1 $1 bill, 1 quarter **2.** $6.25; 1 $5 bill, 1 $1 bill, 1 quarter **3.** $1.25; 1 $1 bill, 1 quarter **4.** $2.00; 2 $1 bills **5.** $.025; 1 quarter **6.** $41.77; 4 $10 bills, 1 $1 bill, 3 quarters, 2 pennies **7.** $11.77; 1 $10 bill, 1 $1 bill, 3 quarters, 2 pennies **8.** $1.77; 1 $1 bill, 3 quarters, 2 pennies **9.** $2.00; 2 $1 bills **10.** $0.77; 3 quarters, 2 pennies

PAGE 80

1. a. 0.7¢ each **b.** 0.5¢ each **c.** 0.3¢ each (best buy)
2. a. 26.3¢ per oz **b.** 25.0¢ per oz **c.** 20.6¢ per oz (best buy)
3. a. 8.3¢ per oz **b.** 7.8¢ per oz (best buy) **c.** 8.9¢ per oz
4. a. 5.8¢ per oz **b.** 4.2¢ per oz (best buy) **c.** 4.4¢ per oz
5. a. 3.0¢ per oz (best buy) **b.** 5.1¢ per oz **c.** 5.4¢ per oz
6. a. 17.4¢ per oz **b.** 15.0¢ per oz (best buy) **c.** 17.2¢ per oz
7. a. 12.9¢ per oz **b.** 12.6¢ per oz (best buy) **c.** 14.5¢ per oz
8. a. 5.1¢ per oz **b.** 3.7¢ per oz **c.** 3.4¢ per oz (best buy)
9. a. 3.2¢ per oz (best buy) **b.** 4.2¢ per oz **c.** 6.2¢ per oz
10. a. 0.4¢ per ft (best buy) **b.** 0.5¢ per ft **c.** 0.6¢ per ft

PAGE 81

1. $34.58; 3 $10 bills, 4 $1 bills, 2 quarters, 1 nickel, 3 pennies **2.** $4.58; 4 $1 bills, 2 quarters, 1 nickel, 3 pennies **3.** $5.00; 1 $5 bill **4.** $0.58; 2 quarters, 1 nickel, 3 pennies **5.** $17.17; 1 $10 bill, 1 $5 bill, 2 $1 bills, 1 dime, 1 nickel, 2 pennies **6.** $13.20; 1 $10 bill, 3 $1 bills, 2 dimes **7.** $3.20; 3 $1 bills, 2 dimes **8.** $5.20; 1 $5 bill, 2 dimes **9.** $5.00; 1 $5 bill **10.** $15.00; 1 $10 bill, 1 $5 bill

PAGE 82

1. a. 9.8¢ per oz **b.** 5.3¢ per oz **c.** 2.5¢ per oz (best buy)
2. a. 9.7¢ each **b.** 9.5¢ each **c.** 7.1¢ each (best buy)
3. a. 79.8¢ per oz (best buy) **b.** 85.6¢ per oz **c.** 82.9¢ per oz
4. a. 3.2¢ each **b.** 2.4¢ each **c.** 1.5¢ each (best buy)
5. a. 43.8¢ per oz **b.** 32.2¢ per oz **c.** 24.9¢ per oz (best buy)
6. a. 1.2¢ each (best buy) **b.** 1.4¢ each **c.** 1.3¢ each
7. a. 15.3¢ per mL **b.** 13.3¢ per mL (best buy) **c.** 14.4¢ per mL
8. a. 6.1¢ each **b.** 4.1¢ each (best buy) **c.** 4.9¢ each
9. a. 8.1¢ per oz **b.** 6.3¢ per oz (best buy) **c.** 6.8¢ per oz
10. a. 3.7¢ per ft^2 **b.** 3.6¢ per ft^2 **c.** 3.3¢ per ft^2 (best buy)

PAGE 83

1. $17.32; 1 $10 bill, 1 $5 bill, 2 $1 bills, 1 quarter, 1 nickel, 2 pennies **2.** $7.32; 1 $5 bill, 2 $1 bills, 1 quarter, 1 nickel, 2 pennies **3.** $2.32; 2 $1 bills, 1 quarter, 1 nickel, 2 pennies **4.** $3.00; 3 $1 bills **5.** $0.32; 1 quarter, 1 nickel, 2 pennies **6.** $11.68; 1 $10 bill, 1 $1 bill, 2 quarters, 1 dime, 1 nickel, 3 pennies **7.** $5.00; 1 $5 bill **8.** $2.00; 2 $1 bills **9.** $1.68; 1 $1 bill, 2 quarters, 1 dime, 1 nickel, 3 pennies **10.** $0.18; 1 dime, 1 nickel, 3 pennies

PAGE 84

1. a. 0.4¢ each **b.** 0.3¢ each (best buy) **c.** 0.5¢ each
2. a. 23.0¢ per oz **b.** 21.8¢ per oz (best buy) **c.** 22.7¢ per oz
3. a. 11.7¢ per oz **b.** 7.8¢ per oz **c.** 7.1¢ per oz (best buy)
4. a. 3.1¢ per oz (best buy) **b.** 4.0¢ per oz **c.** 3.9¢ per oz
5. a. 2.4¢ per oz (best buy) **b.** 3.1¢ per oz **c.** 4.4¢ per oz
6. a. 14.1¢ per oz (best buy) **b.** 14.3¢ per oz **c.** 17.2¢ per oz
7. a. 16.5¢ per oz **b.** 15.3¢ per oz **c.** 14.5¢ per oz (best buy)
8. a. 2.4¢ per oz (best buy) **b.** 3.1¢ per oz **c.** 3.7¢ per oz
9. a. 5.6¢ per oz **b.** 5.0¢ per oz (best buy) **c.** 5.3¢ per oz
10. a. 1.1¢ per ft **b.** 0.9¢ per ft **c.** 0.6¢ per ft (best buy)

PAGE 85

1. $12.43; 1 $10 bill, 2 $1 bills, 1 quarter, 1 dime, 1 nickel, 3 pennies **2.** $5.00; 1 $5 bill **3.** $3.00; 3 $1 bills **4.** $2.43; 2 $1 bills, 1 quarter, 1 dime, 1 nickel, 3 pennies **5.** $0.43; 1 quarter, 1 dime, 1 nickel, 3 pennies **6.** $13.08; 1 $10 bill, 3 $1 bills, 1 nickel, 3 pennies **7.** $3.08; 3 $1 bills, 1 nickel, 3 pennies **8.** $5.00; 1 $5 bill **9.** $4.00; 4 $1 bills **10.** $0.08; 1 nickel, 3 pennies

PAGE 86

1. a. 7.3¢ per oz **b.** 4.9¢ per oz **c.** 2.3¢ per oz (best buy)
2. a. 8.6¢ each **b.** 9.0¢ each **c.** 7.2¢ each (best buy)
3. a. 83.3¢ per oz **b.** 81.3¢ per oz **c.** 70.8¢ per oz (best buy)
4. a. 0.6¢ each (best buy) **b.** 1.0¢ each **c.** 1.2¢ each
5. a. 17.3¢ per oz (best buy) **b.** 26.5¢ per oz **c.** 19.1¢ per oz
6. a. 1.8¢ each **b.** 1.5¢ each (best buy) **c.** 1.6¢ each
7. a. 9.1¢ per mL (best buy) **b.** 9.9¢ per mL **c.** 13.3¢ per mL
8. a. 3.3¢ each **b.** 3.1¢ each (best buy) **c.** 3.6¢ each
9. a. 8.9¢ per oz **b.** 6.5¢ per oz **c.** 4.5¢ per oz (best buy)
10. a. 1.2¢ per ft^2 (best buy) **b.** 2.5¢ per ft^2 **c.** 2.7¢ per ft^2

PAGE 87
1. $17.29; 1 $10 bill, 1 $5 bill, 2 $1 bills, 1 quarter, 4 pennies
2. $7.29; 1 $5 bill, 2 $1 bills, 1 quarter, 4 pennies **3.** $2.29;
2 $1 bills, 1 quarter, 4 pennies **4.** $0.29; 1 quarter, 4 pennies
5. $0.04; 4 pennies **6.** $11.65; 1 $10 bill, 1 $1 bill, 2 quarters,
1 dime, 1 nickel **7.** $1.65; 1 $1 bill, 2 quarters, 1 dime, 1 nickel
8. $0.65; 2 quarters, 1 dime, 1 nickel **9.** $0.15; 1 dime, 1 nickel
10. $0.05; 1 nickel

PAGE 88
1. a. 0.7¢ each **b.** 0.4¢ each **c.** 0.3¢ each (best buy)
2. a. 26.3¢ per oz **b.** 22.0¢ per oz (best buy) **c.** 23.3¢ per oz
3. a. 7.3¢ per oz (best buy) **b.** 8.6¢ per oz **c.** 9.7¢ per oz
4. a. 5.3¢ per oz **b.** 4.3¢ per oz **c.** 3.3¢ per oz (best buy)
5. a. 3.2¢ per oz (best buy) **b.** 4.1¢ per oz **c.** 4.7¢ per oz
6. a. 13.7¢ per oz (best buy) **b.** 14.3¢ per oz **c.** 15.9¢ per oz
7. a. 11.9¢ per oz **b.** 12.1¢ per oz **c.** 11.5¢ per oz
8. a. 4.3¢ per oz **b.** 3.1¢ per oz (best buy) **c.** 3.4¢ per oz
9. a. 2.7¢ per oz (best buy) **b.** 3.1¢ per oz **c.** 5.2¢ per oz
10. a. 0.4¢ per ft (best buy) **b.** 0.7¢ per ft **c.** 0.6¢ per ft

PAGE 89
1. $32.45; 3 $10 bills, 2 $1 bills, 1 quarter, 2 dimes **2.** $2.45;
2 $1 bills, 1 quarter, 2 dimes **3.** $0.45; 1 quarter, 2 dimes **4.** $0.20;
2 dimes **5.** $0.15; 1 dime, 1 nickel **6.** $60.08; 6 $10 bills, 1 nickel,
3 pennies **7.** $10.08; 1 $10 bill, 1 nickel, 3 pennies **8.** $35.08;
3 $10 bills, 1 $5 bill, 1 nickel, 3 pennies **9.** $46.33; 4 $10 bills,
1 $5 bill, 1 $1 bill, 1 quarter, 1 nickel, 3 pennies **10.** $22.58;
2 $10 bills, 2 $1 bills, 2 quarters, 1 nickel, 3 pennies

PAGE 90
1. a. 6.0¢ per oz **b.** 6.6¢ per oz **c.** 3.9¢ per oz (best buy)
2. a. 10.0¢ each **b.** 11.0¢ each **c.** 9.7¢ each (best buy)
3. a. 80.8¢ per oz **b.** 71.1¢ per oz (best buy) **c.** 74.9¢ per oz
4. a. 2.8¢ each **b.** 2.2¢ each **c.** 1.5¢ each (best buy)
5. a. 38.5¢ per oz **b.** 31.5¢ per oz (best buy) **c.** 32.4¢ per oz
6. a. 1.7¢ each **b.** 1.4¢ each (best buy) **c.** 1.5¢ each
7. a. 12.4¢ per mL (best buy) **b.** 13.3¢ per mL **c.** 14.4¢ per mL
8. a. 5.3¢ each **b.** 3.5¢ each (best buy) **c.** 4.0¢ each
9. a. 7.3¢ per oz **b.** 6.3¢ per oz (best buy) **c.** 7.0¢ per oz
10. a. 3.4¢ per ft^2 **b.** 3.1¢ per ft^2 **c.** 3.0¢ per ft^2 (best buy)

PAGE 93
1. 79.5 **2.** 112 students **3.** $9,945.60 **4.** 360 mi **5.** 49¢

PAGE 94
1. c. more than necessary **2. b.** not enough
3. c. more than necessary **4. a.** enough **5. c.** more than necessary

PAGE 95
1. $19\frac{1}{12}$ yd **2.** $4\frac{1}{2}$ ft **3.** $370 **4.** 16 **5.** $180

PAGE 96
1. b. not enough **2. a.** enough **3. b.** not enough
4. c. more than necessary **5. a.** enough

PAGE 97
1. $395 **2.** $7,620 **3.** $4\frac{7}{8}$ cups **4.** $164 **5.** 80 tiles

PAGE 98
1. b. not enough **2. a.** enough **3. a.** enough **4. b.** not enough
5. a. enough

PAGE 99
1. 164 **2.** $39.12 **3.** 22 mph **4.** 3 years **5.** $5\frac{1}{4}$ cups

PAGE 100
1. c. more than necessary **2. c.** more than necessary **3. a.** enough
4. c. more than necessary **5. b.** not enough

PAGE 101
1. $2,235 **2.** $23.70 **3.** $30.30 **4.** 27 points **5.** 34,524 people

PAGE 102
1. a. enough **2. c.** more than necessary **3. b.** not enough
4. b. not enough **5. c.** more than necessary

PAGE 103
1. $48 **2.** 9% **3.** $2\frac{1}{4}$ ft **4.** 336 cans **5.** 17.577 in.

PAGE 104
1. a. 1,600 **2. c.** $1,600 **3. b.** 1,000,000 **4. c.** 55 **5. d.** 20 pounds

PAGE 105
1. 312 papers **2.** 84 carnations **3.** $1,350 **4.** $20.41 **5.** 84

PAGE 106
1. b. 50 **2. b.** 8 m **3. b.** 37,000 **4. a.** 8 minutes **5. c.** $25,000,000

PAGE 107
1. $34.85 **2.** 81 **3.** $2,160 **4.** 80% **5.** $19\frac{1}{4}$ ft

PAGE 108
1. c. $50,000,000,000 **2. d.** 970 feet **3. a.** $40,000 **4. b.** 6,000
5. c. 37

PAGE 109
1. 42 mph **2.** 107 days **3.** $17\frac{7}{8}$ oz **4.** 4 years **5.** $6.25

PAGE 110
1. a. 12 to 1 **2. b.** 37 **3. b.** 7,000 **4. a.** 0.5 second **5. d.** 5,000

PAGE 111
1. 188 people **2.** $8.50 **3.** 12% **4.** 75 gal **5.** $21.78

PAGE 112
1. d. $12,000 **2. c.** 18,000 in^3 **3. b.** 15 **4. a.** 290 **5. c.** $35,000

FEDERAL INCOME TAX TABLE

For use with pages 14, 16, 18, 20, and 22.

If your taxable income is—		And you are—			
At least	But less than	Single	Married filing jointly	Married filing separately	Head of a household
		Your tax is—			

32,000

At least	But less than	Single	Married filing jointly	Married filing separately	Head of a household
32,000	32,050	5,672	4,804	6,214	4,804
32,050	32,100	5,686	4,811	6,228	4,811
32,100	32,150	5,700	4,819	6,242	4,819
32,150	32,200	5,714	4,826	6,256	4,826
32,200	32,250	5,728	4,834	6,270	4,834
32,250	32,300	5,742	4,841	6,284	4,841
32,300	32,350	5,756	4,849	6,298	4,849
32,350	32,400	5,770	4,856	6,312	4,856
32,400	32,450	5,784	4,864	6,326	4,864
32,450	32,500	5,798	4,871	6,340	4,871
32,500	32,550	5,812	4,879	6,354	4,879
32,550	32,600	5,826	4,886	6,368	4,886
32,600	32,650	5,840	4,894	6,382	4,894
32,650	32,700	5,854	4,901	6,396	4,901
32,700	32,750	5,868	4,909	6,410	4,909
32,750	32,800	5,882	4,916	6,424	4,916
32,800	32,850	5,896	4,924	6,438	4,924
32,850	32,900	5,910	4,931	6,452	4,931
32,900	32,950	5,924	4,939	6,466	4,939
32,950	33,000	5,938	4,946	6,480	4,946

33,000

At least	But less than	Single	Married filing jointly	Married filing separately	Head of a household
33,000	33,050	5,952	4,954	6,494	4,954
33,050	33,100	5,966	4,961	6,508	4,961
33,100	33,150	5,980	4,969	6,522	4,969
33,150	33,200	5,994	4,976	6,536	4,976
33,200	33,250	6,008	4,984	6,550	4,984
33,250	33,300	6,022	4,991	6,564	4,991
33,300	33,350	6,036	4,999	6,578	4,999
33,350	33,400	6,050	5,006	6,592	5,006
33,400	33,450	6,064	5,014	6,606	5,014
33,450	33,500	6,078	5,021	6,620	5,021
33,500	33,550	6,092	5,029	6,634	5,029
33,550	33,600	6,106	5,036	6,648	5,036
33,600	33,650	6,120	5,044	6,662	5,044
33,650	33,700	6,134	5,051	6,676	5,051
33,700	33,750	6,148	5,059	6,690	5,059
33,750	33,800	6,162	5,066	6,704	5,066
33,800	33,850	6,176	5,074	6,718	5,074
33,850	33,900	6,190	5,081	6,732	5,081
33,900	33,950	6,204	5,089	6,746	5,089
33,950	34,000	6,218	5,096	6,760	5,100

34,000

At least	But less than	Single	Married filing jointly	Married filing separately	Head of a household
34,000	34,050	6,232	5,104	6,774	5,114
34,050	34,100	6,246	5,111	6,788	5,128
34,100	34,150	6,260	5,119	6,802	5,142
34,150	34,200	6,274	5,126	6,816	5,156
34,200	34,250	6,288	5,134	6,830	5,170
34,250	34,300	6,302	5,141	6,844	5,184
34,300	34,350	6,316	5,149	6,858	5,198
34,350	34,400	6,330	5,156	6,872	5,212
34,400	34,450	6,344	5,164	6,886	5,226
34,450	34,500	6,358	5,171	6,900	5,240
34,500	34,550	6,372	5,179	6,914	5,254
34,550	34,600	6,386	5,186	6,928	5,268
34,600	34,650	6,400	5,194	6,942	5,282
34,650	34,700	6,414	5,201	6,956	5,296
34,700	34,750	6,428	5,209	6,970	5,310
34,750	34,800	6,442	5,216	6,984	5,324
34,800	34,850	6,456	5,224	6,998	5,338
34,850	34,900	6,470	5,231	7,012	5,352
34,900	34,950	6,484	5,239	7,026	5,366
34,950	35,000	6,498	5,246	7,040	5,380

35,000

At least	But less than	Single	Married filing jointly	Married filing separately	Head of a household
35,000	35,050	6,512	5,254	7,054	5,394
35,050	35,100	6,526	5,261	7,068	5,408
35,100	35,150	6,540	5,269	7,082	5,422
35,150	35,200	6,554	5,276	7,096	5,436
35,200	35,250	6,568	5,284	7,110	5,450
35,250	35,300	6,582	5,291	7,124	5,464
35,300	35,350	6,596	5,299	7,138	5,478
35,350	35,400	6,610	5,306	7,152	5,492
35,400	35,450	6,624	5,314	7,166	5,506
35,450	35,500	6,638	5,321	7,180	5,520
35,500	35,550	6,652	5,329	7,194	5,534
35,550	35,600	6,666	5,336	7,208	5,548
35,600	35,650	6,680	5,344	7,222	5,562
35,650	35,700	6,694	5,351	7,236	5,576
35,700	35,750	6,708	5,359	7,250	5,590
35,750	35,800	6,722	5,366	7,264	5,604
35,800	35,850	6,736	5,374	7,278	5,618
35,850	35,900	6,750	5,381	7,292	5,632
35,900	35,950	6,764	5,389	7,306	5,646
35,950	36,000	6,778	5,396	7,320	5,660

36,000

At least	But less than	Single	Married filing jointly	Married filing separately	Head of a household
36,000	36,050	6,792	5,404	7,334	5,674
36,050	36,100	6,806	5,411	7,348	5,688
36,100	36,150	6,820	5,419	7,362	5,702
36,150	36,200	6,834	5,426	7,376	5,716
36,200	36,250	6,848	5,434	7,390	5,730
36,250	36,300	6,862	5,441	7,404	5,744
36,300	36,350	6,876	5,449	7,418	5,758
36,350	36,400	6,890	5,456	7,432	5,772
36,400	36,450	6,904	5,464	7,446	5,786
36,450	36,500	6,918	5,471	7,460	5,800
36,500	36,550	6,932	5,479	7,474	5,814
36,550	36,600	6,946	5,486	7,488	5,828
36,600	36,650	6,960	5,494	7,502	5,842
36,650	36,700	6,974	5,501	7,516	5,856
36,700	36,750	6,988	5,509	7,530	5,870
36,750	36,800	7,002	5,516	7,544	5,884
36,800	36,850	7,016	5,524	7,558	5,898
36,850	36,900	7,030	5,531	7,572	5,912
36,900	36,950	7,044	5,539	7,586	5,926
36,950	37,000	7,058	5,546	7,600	5,940

37,000

At least	But less than	Single	Married filing jointly	Married filing separately	Head of a household
37,000	37,050	7,072	5,554	7,614	5,954
37,050	37,100	7,086	5,561	7,628	5,968
37,100	37,150	7,100	5,569	7,642	5,982
37,150	37,200	7,114	5,576	7,656	5,996
37,200	37,250	7,128	5,584	7,670	6,010
37,250	37,300	7,142	5,591	7,684	6,024
37,300	37,350	7,156	5,599	7,698	6,038
37,350	37,400	7,170	5,606	7,712	6,052
37,400	37,450	7,184	5,614	7,726	6,066
37,450	37,500	7,198	5,621	7,740	6,080
37,500	37,550	7,212	5,629	7,754	6,094
37,550	37,600	7,226	5,636	7,768	6,108
37,600	37,650	7,240	5,644	7,782	6,122
37,650	37,700	7,254	5,651	7,796	6,136
37,700	37,750	7,268	5,659	7,810	6,150
37,750	37,800	7,282	5,666	7,824	6,164
37,800	37,850	7,296	5,674	7,838	6,178
37,850	37,900	7,310	5,681	7,852	6,192
37,900	37,950	7,324	5,689	7,866	6,206
37,950	38,000	7,338	5,696	7,880	6,220

38,000

At least	But less than	Single	Married filing jointly	Married filing separately	Head of a household
38,000	38,050	7,352	5,704	7,894	6,234
38,050	38,100	7,366	5,711	7,908	6,248
38,100	38,150	7,380	5,719	7,922	6,262
38,150	38,200	7,394	5,726	7,936	6,276
38,200	38,250	7,408	5,734	7,950	6,290
38,250	38,300	7,422	5,741	7,964	6,304
38,300	38,350	7,436	5,749	7,978	6,318
38,350	38,400	7,450	5,756	7,992	6,332
38,400	38,450	7,464	5,764	8,006	6,346
38,450	38,500	7,478	5,771	8,020	6,360
38,500	38,550	7,492	5,779	8,034	6,374
38,550	38,600	7,506	5,786	8,048	6,388
38,600	38,650	7,520	5,794	8,062	6,402
38,650	38,700	7,534	5,801	8,076	6,416
38,700	38,750	7,548	5,809	8,090	6,430
38,750	38,800	7,562	5,816	8,104	6,444
38,800	38,850	7,576	5,824	8,118	6,458
38,850	38,900	7,590	5,831	8,132	6,472
38,900	38,950	7,604	5,839	8,146	6,486
38,950	39,000	7,618	5,846	8,160	6,500

39,000

At least	But less than	Single	Married filing jointly	Married filing separately	Head of a household
39,000	39,050	7,632	5,854	8,174	6,514
39,050	39,100	7,646	5,861	8,188	6,528
39,100	39,150	7,660	5,869	8,202	6,542
39,150	39,200	7,674	5,876	8,216	6,556
39,200	39,250	7,688	5,884	8,230	6,570
39,250	39,300	7,702	5,891	8,244	6,584
39,300	39,350	7,716	5,899	8,258	6,598
39,350	39,400	7,730	5,906	8,272	6,612
39,400	39,450	7,744	5,914	8,286	6,626
39,450	39,500	7,758	5,921	8,300	6,640
39,500	39,550	7,772	5,929	8,314	6,654
39,550	39,600	7,786	5,936	8,328	6,668
39,600	39,650	7,800	5,944	8,342	6,682
39,650	39,700	7,814	5,951	8,356	6,696
39,700	39,750	7,828	5,959	8,370	6,710
39,750	39,800	7,842	5,966	8,384	6,724
39,800	39,850	7,856	5,974	8,398	6,738
39,850	39,900	7,870	5,981	8,412	6,752
39,900	39,950	7,884	5,989	8,426	6,766
39,950	40,000	7,898	5,996	8,440	6,780

40,000

At least	But less than	Single	Married filing jointly	Married filing separately	Head of a household
40,000	40,050	7,912	6,004	8,454	6,794
40,050	40,100	7,926	6,011	8,468	6,808
40,100	40,150	7,940	6,019	8,482	6,822
40,150	40,200	7,954	6,026	8,496	6,836
40,200	40,250	7,968	6,034	8,510	6,850
40,250	40,300	7,982	6,041	8,524	6,864
40,300	40,350	7,996	6,049	8,538	6,878
40,350	40,400	8,010	6,056	8,552	6,892
40,400	40,450	8,024	6,064	8,566	6,906
40,450	40,500	8,038	6,071	8,580	6,920
40,500	40,550	8,052	6,079	8,594	6,934
40,550	40,600	8,066	6,086	8,608	6,948
40,600	40,650	8,080	6,094	8,622	6,962
40,650	40,700	8,094	6,101	8,636	6,976
40,700	40,750	8,108	6,109	8,650	6,990
40,750	40,800	8,122	6,116	8,664	7,004
40,800	40,850	8,136	6,124	8,678	7,018
40,850	40,900	8,150	6,131	8,692	7,032
40,900	40,950	8,164	6,139	8,706	7,046
40,950	41,000	8,178	6,146	8,720	7,060

Basic Computation Series 2000: Applying Computational Skills
TABLES AND MAPS

STATE INCOME TAX TABLE

For use with pages 14, 16, 18, 20, and 22.

TAXABLE INCOME Over	But not over	TAX
25,510	25,610	1,278
25,610	25,710	1,283
25,710	25,810	1,288
25,810	25,910	1,293
25,910	26,010	1,298
26,010	26,110	1,303
26,110	26,210	1,308
26,210	26,310	1,313
26,310	26,410	1,318
26,410	26,510	1,323
26,510	26,610	1,328
26,610	26,710	1,333
26,710	26,810	1,338
26,810	26,910	1,343
26,910	27,010	1,348
27,010	27,110	1,353
27,110	27,210	1,358
27,210	27,310	1,363
27,310	27,410	1,368
27,410	27,510	1,373
27,510	27,610	1,378
27,610	27,710	1,383
27,710	27,810	1,388
27,810	27,910	1,393
27,910	28,010	1,398
28,010	28,110	1,403
28,110	28,210	1,408
28,210	28,310	1,413
28,310	28,410	1,418
28,410	28,510	1,423
28,510	28,610	1,428
28,610	28,710	1,433
28,710	28,810	1,438
28,810	28,910	1,443
28,910	29,010	1,448
29,010	29,110	1,453
29,110	29,210	1,458
29,210	29,310	1,463
29,310	29,410	1,468
29,410	29,510	1,473
29,510	29,610	1,478
29,610	29,710	1,483
29,710	29,810	1,488
29,810	29,910	1,493
29,910	30,010	1,498
30,010	30,110	1,503
30,110	30,210	1,508
30,210	30,310	1,513
30,310	30,410	1,518
30,410	30,510	1,523
30,510	30,610	1,528
30,610	30,710	1,533
30,710	30,810	1,538
30,810	30,910	1,543
30,910	31,010	1,548

TAXABLE INCOME Over	But not over	TAX
31,010	31,110	1,553
31,110	31,210	1,558
31,210	31,310	1,563
31,310	31,410	1,568
31,410	31,510	1,573
31,510	31,610	1,578
31,610	31,710	1,583
31,710	31,810	1,588
31,810	31,910	1,593
31,910	32,010	1,598
32,010	32,110	1,603
32,110	32,210	1,608
32,210	32,310	1,613
32,310	32,410	1,618
32,410	32,510	1,623
32,510	32,610	1,628
32,610	32,710	1,633
32,710	32,810	1,638
32,810	32,910	1,643
32,910	33,010	1,648
33,010	33,110	1,653
33,110	33,210	1,658
33,210	33,310	1,663
33,310	33,410	1,668
33,410	33,510	1,673
33,510	33,610	1,678
33,610	33,710	1,683
33,710	33,810	1,688
33,810	33,910	1,693
33,910	34,010	1,698
34,010	34,110	1,703
34,110	34,210	1,708
34,210	34,310	1,713
34,310	34,410	1,718
34,410	34,510	1,723
34,510	34,610	1,728
34,610	34,710	1,733
34,710	34,810	1,738
34,810	34,910	1,743
34,910	35,010	1,748
35,010	35,110	1,753
35,110	35,210	1,758
35,210	35,310	1,763
35,310	35,410	1,768
35,410	35,510	1,773
35,510	35,610	1,778
35,610	35,710	1,783
35,710	35,810	1,788
35,810	35,910	1,793
35,910	36,010	1,798
36,010	36,110	1,803
36,110	36,210	1,808
36,210	36,310	1,813
36,310	36,410	1,818
36,410	36,510	1,823

TAXABLE INCOME Over	But not over	TAX
36,510	36,610	1,828
36,610	36,710	1,833
36,710	36,810	1,838
36,810	36,910	1,843
36,910	37,010	1,848
37,010	37,110	1,853
37,110	37,210	1,858
37,210	37,310	1,863
37,310	37,410	1,868
37,410	37,510	1,873
37,510	37,610	1,878
37,610	37,710	1,883
37,710	37,810	1,888
37,810	37,910	1,893
37,910	38,010	1,898
38,010	38,110	1,903
38,110	38,210	1,908
38,210	38,310	1,913
38,310	38,410	1,918
38,410	38,510	1,923
38,510	38,610	1,928
38,610	38,710	1,933
38,710	38,810	1,938
38,810	38,910	1,943
38,910	39,010	1,948
39,010	39,110	1,953
39,110	39,210	1,958
39,210	39,310	1,963
39,310	39,410	1,968
39,410	39,510	1,973
39,510	39,610	1,978
39,610	39,710	1,983
39,710	39,810	1,988
39,810	39,910	1,993
39,910	40,010	1,998
40,010	40,110	2,003
40,110	40,210	2,008
40,210	40,310	2,013
40,310	40,410	2,018
40,410	40,510	2,023
40,510	40,610	2,028
40,610	40,710	2,033
40,710	40,810	2,038
40,810	40,910	2,043
40,910	41,010	2,048
41,010	41,110	2,053
41,110	41,210	2,058
41,210	41,310	2,063
41,310	41,410	2,068
41,410	41,510	2,073
41,510	41,610	2,078
41,610	41,710	2,083
41,710	41,810	2,088
41,810	41,910	2,093
41,910	42,010	2,098

TAXABLE INCOME Over	But not over	TAX
42,010	42,110	2,103
42,110	42,210	2,108
42,210	42,310	2,113
42,310	42,410	2,118
42,410	42,510	2,123
42,510	42,610	2,128
42,610	42,710	2,133
42,710	42,810	2,138
42,810	42,910	2,143
42,910	43,010	2,148
43,010	43,110	2,153
43,110	43,210	2,158
43,210	43,310	2,163
43,310	43,410	2,168
43,410	43,510	2,173
43,510	43,610	2,178
43,610	43,710	2,183
43,710	43,810	2,188
43,810	43,910	2,193
43,910	44,010	2,198
44,010	44,110	2,203
44,110	44,210	2,208
44,210	44,310	2,213
44,310	44,410	2,218
44,410	44,510	2,223
44,510	44,610	2,228
44,610	44,710	2,233
44,710	44,810	2,238
44,810	44,910	2,243
44,910	45,010	2,248
45,010	45,110	2,253
45,110	45,210	2,258
45,210	45,310	2,263
45,310	45,410	2,268
45,410	45,510	2,273
45,510	45,610	2,278
45,610	45,710	2,283
45,710	45,810	2,288
45,810	45,910	2,293
45,910	46,010	2,298

TAXABLE INCOME Over	But not over	TAX
46,010	46,110	2,303
46,110	46,210	2,308
46,210	46,310	2,313
46,310	46,410	2,318
46,410	46,510	2,323
46,510	46,610	2,328
46,610	46,710	2,333
46,710	46,810	2,338
46,810	46,910	2,343
46,910	47,010	2,348
47,010	47,110	2,353
47,110	47,210	2,358
47,210	47,310	2,363
47,310	47,410	2,368
47,410	47,510	2,373
47,510	47,610	2,378
47,610	47,710	2,383
47,710	47,810	2,388
47,810	47,910	2,393
47,910	48,010	2,398
48,010	48,110	2,403
48,110	48,210	2,408
48,210	48,310	2,413
48,310	48,410	2,418
48,410	48,510	2,423
48,510	48,610	2,428
48,610	48,710	2,433
48,710	48,810	2,438
48,810	48,910	2,443
48,910	49,010	2,448
49,010	49,110	2,453
49,110	49,210	2,458
49,210	49,310	2,463
49,310	49,410	2,468
49,410	49,510	2,473
49,510	49,610	2,478
49,610	49,710	2,483
49,710	49,810	2,488
49,810	49,910	2,493
49,910	50,010	2,498

SALES TAX TABLE

For use with pages 14, 16, 18, 20, and 22.

$6\frac{1}{2}$% TAX SCHEDULE

Transaction	Tax	Transaction	Tax	Transaction	Tax
25.31–25.46	1.65	33.77–33.92	2.20	42.24–42.38	2.75
25.47–25.61	1.66	33.93–34.07	2.21	42.39–42.53	2.76
25.62–25.76	1.67	34.08–34.23	2.22	42.54–42.69	2.77
25.77–25.91	1.68	34.24–34.38	2.23	42.70–42.84	2.78
25.92–26.07	1.69	34.39–34.53	2.24	42.85–42.99	2.79
26.08–26.23	1.70	34.54–34.69	2.25	43.00–43.15	2.80
26.24–26.38	1.71	34.70–34.84	2.26	43.16–43.30	2.81
26.39–26.53	1.72	34.85–34.99	2.27	43.31–43.46	2.82
26.54–26.69	1.73	35.00–35.15	2.28	43.47–43.61	2.83
26.70–26.84	1.74	35.16–35.30	2.29	43.62–43.76	2.84
26.85–26.99	1.75	35.31–35.46	2.30	43.77–43.92	2.85
27.00–27.15	1.76	35.47–35.61	2.31	43.93–44.07	2.86
27.16–27.30	1.77	35.62–35.76	2.32	44.08–44.23	2.87
27.31–27.46	1.78	35.77–35.92	2.33	44.24–44.38	2.88
27.47–27.61	1.79	35.93–36.07	2.34	44.39–44.53	2.89
27.62–27.76	1.80	36.08–36.23	2.35	44.54–44.69	2.90
27.77–27.92	1.81	36.24–36.38	2.36	44.70–44.84	2.91
27.93–28.07	1.82	36.39–36.53	2.37	44.85–44.99	2.92
28.08–28.23	1.83	36.54–36.69	2.38	45.00–45.15	2.93
28.24–28.38	1.84	36.70–36.84	2.39	45.16–45.30	2.94
28.39–28.53	1.85	36.85–36.99	2.40	45.31–45.46	2.95
28.54–28.69	1.86	37.00–37.15	2.41	45.47–45.61	2.96
28.70–28.84	1.87	37.16–37.30	2.42	45.62–45.76	2.97
28.85–28.99	1.88	37.31–37.46	2.43	45.77–45.92	2.98
29.00–29.15	1.89	37.47–37.61	2.44	45.93–46.07	2.99
29.16–29.30	1.90	37.62–37.76	2.45	46.08–46.23	3.00
29.31–29.46	1.91	37.77–37.92	2.46	46.24–46.38	3.01
29.47–29.61	1.92	37.93–38.07	2.47	46.39–46.53	3.02
29.62–29.76	1.93	38.08–38.23	2.48	46.54–46.69	3.03
29.77–29.92	1.94	38.24–38.38	2.49	46.70–46.84	3.04
29.93–30.07	1.95	38.39–38.53	2.50	46.85–46.99	3.05
30.08–30.23	1.96	38.54–38.69	2.51	47.00–47.15	3.06
30.24–30.38	1.97	38.70–38.84	2.52	47.16–47.30	3.07
30.39–30.53	1.98	38.85–38.99	2.53	47.31–47.46	3.08
30.54–30.69	1.99	39.00–39.15	2.54	47.47–47.61	3.09
30.70–30.84	2.00	39.16–39.30	2.55	47.62–47.76	3.10
30.85–30.99	2.01	39.31–39.46	2.56	47.77–47.92	3.11
31.00–31.15	2.02	39.47–39.61	2.57	47.93–48.07	3.12
31.16–31.30	2.03	39.62–39.76	2.58	48.08–48.23	3.13
31.31–31.46	2.04	39.77–39.92	2.59	48.24–48.38	3.14
31.47–31.61	2.05	39.93–40.07	2.60	48.39–48.53	3.15
31.62–31.76	2.06	40.08–40.23	2.61	48.54–48.69	3.16
31.77–31.92	2.07	40.24–40.38	2.62	48.70–48.84	3.17
31.93–32.07	2.08	40.39–40.53	2.63	48.85–48.99	3.18
32.08–32.23	2.09	40.54–40.69	2.64	49.00–49.15	3.19
32.24–32.38	2.10	40.70–40.84	2.65	49.16–49.30	3.20
32.39–32.53	2.11	40.85–40.99	2.66	49.31–49.46	3.21
32.54–32.69	2.12	41.00–41.15	2.67	49.47–49.61	3.22
32.70–32.84	2.13	41.16–41.30	2.68	49.62–49.76	3.23
32.85–32.99	2.14	41.31–41.46	2.69	49.77–49.92	3.24
33.00–33.15	2.15	41.47–41.61	2.70	49.93–50.07	3.25
33.16–33.30	2.16	41.62–41.76	2.71	50.08–50.23	3.26
33.31–33.46	2.17	41.77–41.92	2.72	50.24–50.38	3.27
33.47–33.61	2.18	41.93–42.07	2.73	50.39–50.53	3.28
33.62–33.76	2.19	42.08–42.23	2.74	50.54–50.69	3.29

Basic Computation Series 2000: Applying Computational Skills

TABLES AND MAPS

SQUARES AND SQUARE ROOTS TABLE

For use with pages 15, 17, 19, 21, and 23.

number	square	square root	number	square	square root	number	square	square root
1	1	1	51	2,601	7.141	101	10,201	10.050
2	4	1.414	52	2,704	7.211	102	10,404	10.100
3	9	1.732	53	2,809	7.280	103	10,609	10.149
4	16	2	54	2,916	7.348	104	10,816	10.198
5	25	2.236	55	3,025	7.416	105	11,025	10.247
6	36	2.449	56	3,136	7.483	106	11,236	10.296
7	49	2.646	57	3,249	7.550	107	11,449	10.344
8	64	2.828	58	3,364	7.616	108	11,664	10.392
9	81	3	59	3,481	7.681	109	11,881	10.440
10	100	3.162	60	3,600	7.746	110	12,100	10.488
11	121	3.317	61	3,721	7.810	111	12,321	10.536
12	144	3.464	62	3,844	7.874	112	12,544	10.583
13	169	3.606	63	3,969	7.937	113	12,769	10.630
14	196	3.742	64	4,096	8	114	12,996	10.677
15	225	3.873	65	4,225	8.062	115	13,225	10.724
16	256	4	66	4,356	8.124	116	13,456	10.770
17	289	4.123	67	4,489	8.185	117	13,689	10.817
18	324	4.243	68	4,624	8.246	118	13,924	10.863
19	361	4.359	69	4,761	8.307	119	14,161	10.909
20	400	4.472	70	4,900	8.367	120	14,400	10.954
21	441	4.583	71	5,041	8.426	121	14,641	11
22	484	4.690	72	5,184	8.485	122	14,884	11.045
23	529	4.796	73	5,329	8.544	123	15,129	11.091
24	576	4.899	74	5,476	8.602	124	15,376	11.136
25	625	5	75	5,625	8.660	125	15,625	11.180
26	676	5.099	76	5,776	8.718	126	15,876	11.225
27	729	5.196	77	5,929	8.775	127	16,129	11.269
28	784	5.292	78	6,084	8.832	128	16,384	11.314
29	841	5.385	79	6,241	8.888	129	16,641	11.358
30	900	5.477	80	6,400	8.944	130	16,900	11.402
31	961	5.568	81	6,561	9	131	17,161	11.446
32	1,024	5.657	82	6,724	9.055	132	17,424	11.489
33	1,089	5.745	83	6,889	9.110	133	17,689	11.533
34	1,156	5.831	84	7,056	9.165	134	17,956	11.576
35	1,225	5.916	85	7,225	9.220	135	18,225	11.619
36	1,296	6	86	7,396	9.274	136	18,496	11.662
37	1,369	6.083	87	7,569	9.327	137	18,769	11.705
38	1,444	6.164	88	7,744	9.381	138	19,044	11.747
39	1,521	6.245	89	7,921	9.434	139	19,321	11.790
40	1,600	6.325	90	8,100	9.487	140	19,600	11.832
41	1,681	6.403	91	8,281	9.539	141	19,881	11.874
42	1,764	6.481	92	8,464	9.592	142	20,164	11.916
43	1,849	6.557	93	8,649	9.644	143	20,449	11.958
44	1,936	6.633	94	8,836	9.695	144	20,736	12
45	2,025	6.708	95	9,025	9.747	145	21,025	12.042
46	2,116	6.782	96	9,216	9.798	146	21,316	12.083
47	2,209	6.856	97	9,409	9.849	147	21,609	12.124
48	2,304	6.928	98	9,604	9.899	148	21,904	12.166
49	2,401	7	99	9,801	9.950	149	22,201	12.207
50	2,500	7.071	100	10,000	10	150	22,500	12.247

MAP OF LINCOLN COUNTY

For use with pages 59–68.
10 mm = 25 km

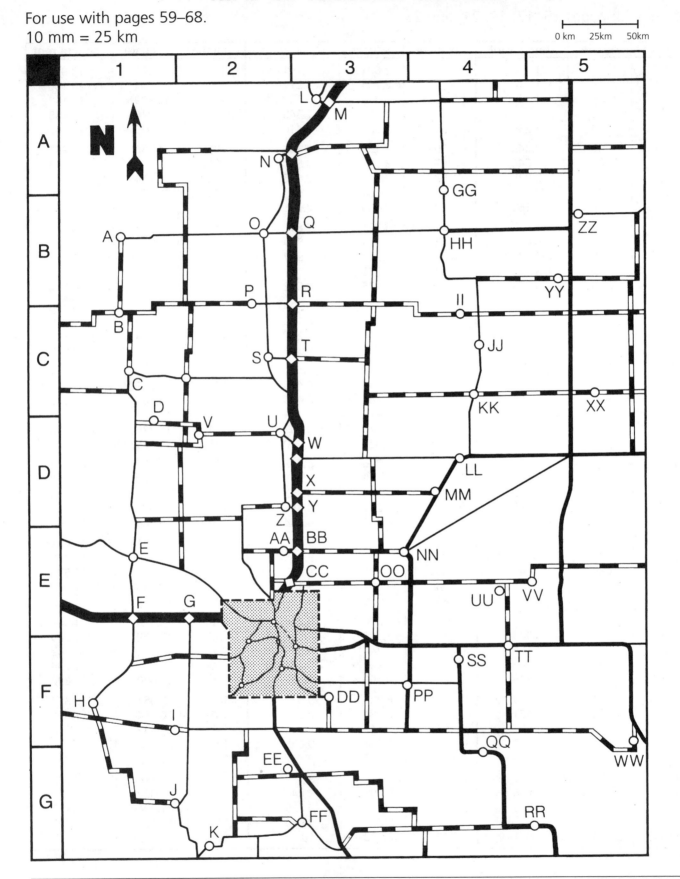

0 km 25km 50km

Basic Computation Series 2000: Applying Computational Skills
TABLES AND MAPS